Anna,

It has been such an amazing summer with you around. You have been such a blessing to the GAMe community and will be sorely missed. I hope this devotional helps you over the next year and that your relationship with God becomes even more intimate. I do hope that God brings blessings & healing to anything that you have been facing in life. Below is my favorite verse; I hope that you will be able to take solace in it as much as I have.

"I consider that our present sufferings are not worth comparing with the glory that will be revealed in us."

Romans 8:18

With love & prayers,

Meredith

Presented to:

Anna Chee

From:

Great Adventures Ministry & Friends

Date:

August 8th, 2019

Embraced

100 DEVOTIONS

to Know God Is

Holding You Close

Lysa TerKeurst

THOMAS NELSON
Since 1798

Published in Nashville, Tennessee, by Thomas Nelson. Thomas Nelson is a registered trademark of HarperCollins Christian Publishing, Inc.

Thomas Nelson titles may be purchased in bulk for educational, business, fund-raising, or sales promotional use. For information, please e-mail SpecialMarkets@ThomasNelson.com.

Unless otherwise noted, Scripture quotations are taken from the Holy Bible, New International Version®, NIV®. Copyright © 1973, 1978, 1984, 2011 by Biblica, Inc.® Used by permission of Zondervan. All rights reserved worldwide. www.zondervan.com. The "NIV" and "New International Version" are trademarks registered in the United States Patent and Trademark Office by Biblica, Inc.®

Scripture quotations marked ESV are from the ESV® Bible (The Holy Bible, English Standard Version®). Copyright © 2001 by Crossway, a publishing ministry of Good News Publishers. Used by permission. All rights reserved.

Scripture quotations marked HCSB are from the Holman Christian Standard Bible®. Copyright © 1999, 2000, 2002, 2003, 2009 by Holman Bible Publishers. Used by permission. HCSB® is a federally registered trademark of Holman Bible Publishers.

Scripture quotations marked NASB are from the New American Standard Bible®, Copyright © 1960, 1962, 1963, 1968, 1971, 1972, 1973, 1975, 1977, 1995 by The Lockman Foundation. Used by permission. (www.Lockman.org)

Scripture quotations marked NKJV are from the New King James Version®. © 1982 by Thomas Nelson. Used by permission. All rights reserved.

Scripture quotations marked NLT are from the *Holy Bible*, New Living Translation. © 1996, 2004, 2007, 2013, 2015 by Tyndale House Foundation. Used by permission of Tyndale House Publishers, Inc., Carol Stream, Illinois 60188. All rights reserved.

Scripture quotations marked THE VOICE are from The Voice™. © 2012 by Ecclesia Bible Society. Used by permission. All rights reserved. Note: Italics in quotations from The Voice are used to "indicate words not directly tied to the dynamic translation of the original language" but that "bring out the nuance of the original, assist in completing ideas, and . . . provide readers with information that would have been obvious to the original audience" (*The Voice*, preface).

Any Internet addresses, phone numbers, or company or product information printed in this book are offered as a resource and are not intended in any way to be or to imply an endorsement by Thomas Nelson, nor does Thomas Nelson vouch for the existence, content, or services of these sites, phone numbers, companies, or products beyond the life of this book.

ISBN 978-1-4003-1030-2 (eBook)

Library of Congress Cataloging-in-Publication Data

ISBN 978-1-4003-1029-6 (HC)

Printed in China

18 19 20 21 22   DSC   15 14 13 12 11 10 9 8 7 6

To anyone who has ever tried to give love without being embraced in return, I understand. But that's exactly why we must know the One who will always fully embrace us and never hold back. My greatest prayer is that as you read these pages you'll know even more deeply that you are loved, cherished, and so intimately cared for by your Heavenly Father.

CONTENTS

CONTENTS

Part 2: Embracing the Fullness Found Only in Him

Part 3: Embracing Him in the Midst of Hurt & Heartbreak

CONTENTS

Part 4: Embracing His Call to Be Transformed

A Note from Lysa

Hi friend,

What an honor it is to meet with you through the typed-out encouragement found in these pages. I want to be that friend who comes alongside you no matter what situation you may find yourself in. I pray you feel the loving embrace of Jesus become more and more real with the turn of every page.

I know it's not always easy for God's voice to rise above all the chaotic noise competing for your heart's attention. The fears. The worries. The hurts and betrayals. The struggle you've begged God to take away that's screaming at you right this very minute. The seemingly easy and perfect lives others post about that pierce your heart with fresh reminders of your hard realities. Your doubts when you have to make a decision that makes almost every path seem increasingly unstable while the Lord seems shockingly quiet. Your secret sorrows that you haven't dared whisper to anyone else about.

Your imperfections feel like neon signs welcoming others' judgments and opinions. Maybe they are real rejections or just simply perceived ones. Either way, every insecure thought is laced with toxic comparison, disappointment, and discouragement.

I know each of these scenarios well because I face them too. And I have to confess that none of this is easy. But the Lord has been so faithful to draw me closer through it all. I think we underestimate how much courage it takes to actually release our desire to fix everything and make the choice to fix our eyes on Jesus.

That's what these devotions are about. They're a glimpse into my own personal journey as I've set out to live the "embraced" life. One where I not only *receive* His embrace, but I *return* His embrace. Embracing His grace, His wisdom, and His rest. Embracing His love, His Word, and His plans. Even embracing the parts of His plan that I find horribly difficult in the moment but completely necessary in the end. Parts that ask me to sacrifice and lay down my own desires and fleshly responses.

You'll quickly realize that I don't do any of this perfectly. But I'm making imperfect progress toward living embraced and embracing at the same time. And something tells me this is how you want to live as well.

If that's true for you, you're in the right place. Rest assured, I'll have tissues and a whispered "Me too" for the hard moments. But you can also count on me for a laugh, slight eye roll, and a "have mercy" for the other everyday moments we'll face.

So if you're ready to start this journey, let's link arms. Fix our gaze on the only One who can direct our steps. And turn the page together.

Sweet Blessings,

Part 1

Embracing the Pursuit of Him and His Direction

1

GIVING MY FIRST MOMENTS TO GOD

Teach me your way, LORD,
    that I may rely on your faithfulness;
give me an undivided heart,
    that I may fear your name.
—PSALM 86:11

*I*t is very early in the morning. Though my body begs me to go back to sleep, my soul stirs to get up and talk with Jesus.

And though I can't physically see Him, I know He is present.

I open my Bible to the book of Psalms and pray through the verses I read to start my day. The more I do this, the less I hear the ongoing naggings of this world. A beautiful melody of God's truth rises up, and my worries fade in their light.

His perspective on what troubles me overshadows my anxiety. This time alone with God prepares me for what I will need throughout the day. He's equipping me to handle what is ahead with His gentle boldness, quiet strength, and loving grace.

In Psalm 81:10, God instructs me, "Open wide your mouth and I will fill it."

He will give me what to say. What to say in happy moments and in aggravating moments. What to say when I feel insecure and what to say when I am confident.

He also reminds me that sometimes it is good to keep my mouth closed and say nothing at all.

I want it to be evident that I'm a girl who spends time with Jesus and that He's working on me.

Psalm 84:1 reminds me that God's dwelling place is lovely. So I ask for Him to dwell in me richly. I want it to be evident that I'm a girl who spends time with Jesus and that He's working on me—shifting a wrong attitude, guarding my words, and whispering constant truths into my heart.

Psalm 86:11 prompts me to request, "Teach me your way, LORD, that I may rely on your faithfulness; give me an undivided heart, that I may fear your name."

Each of these verses leads my morning prayer:

Lord, may nothing separate me from You today. Teach me how to choose only Your way today so each step will lead me closer to You. Help me walk by Your Word and not my feelings.

Help me to keep my heart pure and undivided. Protect me from my own careless thoughts, words, and actions. And keep me from being distracted by MY wants, MY desires, MY thoughts on how things should be.

Help me to embrace what comes my way as an opportunity . . . rather than a personal inconvenience.

And finally, help me to rest in the truth of Psalm 86:13, "Great is your love toward me."

You already see the ways I will fall short and mess up. But right now, I consciously tuck Your whisper of absolute love for me into the deepest part of my heart. I recognize Your love for me is not based on my performance. You love me . . . shortcomings and all.

That's amazing.

But what's most amazing is that the Savior of the world would desire a few minutes with me this morning. Lord, help me to forever remember what a gift it is to sit with You like this. In Jesus' Name, Amen.

I'm now ready to face today. Armed with truth. Surrounded by love. Filled with gratitude.

Dear Lord, I love You. All that I've expressed above is the desire of my heart. I confess that sometimes my actions and reactions betray my love for You. Please forgive me. Thank You for Your grace that enables me to recognize this new day as a new chance to walk closer with You. In Jesus' Name, Amen.

2

THE PINEAPPLE PRINCIPLE

> Get rid of all moral filth and the evil that is so
> prevalent and humbly accept the word planted in
> you, which can save you. Do not merely listen to the
> word, and so deceive yourselves. Do what it says.
>
> —JAMES 1:21–22

I love fresh-cut pineapple. I love the way it tastes. I love that it has no fat grams. And I love that it can be served at any meal—breakfast, lunch, or dinner—as the perfect, healthy side dish.

The problem with fresh pineapples is that they are slightly complicated. To hold up a fresh pineapple and look upon it longingly can be quite frustrating when you haven't a clue how to properly cut it open. So, for years I would walk by the fresh pineapples in the grocery store produce section, heave a sigh, and head straight to the canned fruit aisle. The canned version was fine in a pinch but honestly didn't compare to the fresh. It simply teased my taste buds that greater possibilities existed.

Then one day a friend I was visiting asked me if I'd like a snack. I gasped when she brought out a real pineapple. With ease she turned the fruit on its side and chopped off the top and the bottom. Then she sat it upright on its level end and proceeded to cut sections from each side, starting at the edge of the core. She then shaved off the outer skin, chopped the fruit into bite-sized pieces, and handed me a whole bowlful.

I was amazed. That's it? That's all there is to it? You mean for years I've missed out on the goodness of fresh pineapples because I couldn't figure out how to do *that*?

For years, I took the same approach with studying the Bible as I did with the pineapple. I looked at biblical truth from afar. I didn't feel equipped to open it and study it on my own. Instead of reading the fresh truth for myself, I only read books that talked *about* the Bible. Just like that canned pineapple, my experience with learning God's truth teased me that greater possibilities existed. But since I had no idea how to get them for myself, I avoided the Bible and settled for whatever I could glean from other people.

Then I attended a Bible study in which the teacher modeled how to open up the Bible and study it for ourselves. Each week I watched her dig into Scriptures with a passion and hunger for truth that I'd never known. The way she put verses into context and brought out the meanings from the original text amazed me.

Slowly, I decided to try it for myself. I started getting into God's Word so it could get into me. I no longer wanted to simply settle for learning facts about the Bible when it was meant for so much more. I wanted God's Word to interrupt me, change me, and satisfy me. And that meant not only reading and studying the Bible but also developing the habit of living out its message in my everyday life.

The apostle James addresses this in our key verses: "Get rid of all moral filth and the evil that is so prevalent and

I started getting into God's Word so it could get into me.

humbly accept the word planted in you, which can save you. Do not merely listen to the word, and so deceive yourselves. Do what it says" (James 1:21–22).

The more we make a habit of applying God's Word to our lives, the more it becomes part of our nature—our natural way of acting and reacting. Knowing God's Word and doing what it says not only helps us while going through heartbreak and trouble, it also brings more satisfaction to our souls than anything else ever could.

Thank You, Lord, for giving us good things to nourish us in body and soul. Help me to dig in to Your Word and let it become part of me. In Jesus' Name, Amen.

3

Stop Reading Your Bible

Give me understanding and I will obey your instructions;
I will put them into practice with all my heart.
—Psalm 119:34 NLT

I have a request today. One that might sound odd right after reading the first two devotions: stop reading your Bible.

Does that shock you? Relieve you? Make you angry at worst? Curious at best?

Read on, and see what I mean by this request.

There have been many days in my Christian journey when God was reduced to something on my to-do list. Somewhere along the way, I picked up an unwritten checklist of sorts explaining what "good Christians" are supposed to do:

Pray.
Read your Bible.
Go to church.
Don't cuss.
Be nice.

Being the rule-following girl I am, I subscribed to the good things on that list and waited with great expectations to receive the zap of contentment and happiness good Christian girls are supposed to exude.

But then something felt wrong with me. I still felt restless. I still reacted in anger. I still felt a bit hollow.

I was going through all the motions but didn't feel connected to Jesus. Others around me seemed very connected. They would talk of being "moved by the Spirit." They would hear from God Himself. They would clap their hands and shout "Amen" in the middle of a sermon that sounded like Greek to me.

I often felt like a weightless soul grasping at the air, hoping to somehow snag this Jesus that was just out of reach. Have you ever been there?

This nagging sense creeps in that you'll never get it—that you don't have what it takes to be a Christian. That's where I was. I lived there for a long time until someone challenged me to stop simply reading my Bible because it was a thing on my Christian checklist. Instead, they challenged me to experience God. To know God.

In other words, I needed to look at the words in the Bible as a love letter. God's love letter to a broken-down girl. A love letter not meant to simply be read . . . but a love letter meant to be *lived*.

I won't lie. It took a while.

It took many days of sitting down with my Bible while praying gut-honest prayers. I told God I wasn't connecting. I told Him I wanted to understand, just like the psalmist in our key verse, Psalm 119:34.

I asked Him to help me. I begged Him to help me. Finally, one verse came alive to me. I literally felt moved when I read it. I memorized it and thought about it all day long. All week long. Maybe all month long.

I was overjoyed. I had a verse. A verse where Jesus spoke tenderly and clearly and specifically to me. It was Jeremiah 29:11, "'I know the plans I have for you,' declares the LORD, 'plans to prosper you and not to harm you, plans to give you hope and a future.'"

Slowly, I added more verses. Day by day. Chapter by chapter. And eventually my Bible became my greatest treasure, my love letter.

Now, every day I open up God's Word with great expectation and intentionally look for my verse for that day. Usually one verse among the many I read during my devotion time grabs my heart, and I know it's meant just for the day ahead. And then I attempt to live that verse out in some way, that very day.

When I make the connection between what happens in my life that day and why I need that verse, I experience God.

When I make the connection between what happens in my life that day and why I need that verse, I experience God. I see Him active in my life, and I become even more deeply aware of His constant presence.

I'm sure some Bible scholars would probably take issue with my simplistic approach, but it sure has helped me.

So, back to my original statement. Stop reading your Bible. In other words, *stop simply reading it because you have to cross it off the Christian checklist.*

Instead, read it with great expectations of connecting more deeply and living more authentically with God.

Dear Lord, thank You for showing me the Christian life can be so much more than a checklist. I want to not only read Your Word, but live it out each day. Please give me the wisdom to understand and the courage to become more like You. In Jesus' Name, Amen.

4

GREAT SERMONS AREN'T PREACHED, THEY'RE LIVED

All Scripture is God-breathed and is useful for teaching, rebuking, correcting and training in righteousness, so that the servant of God may be thoroughly equipped for every good work.

—2 TIMOTHY 3:16–17

What if someone followed me around with a video camera all day documenting my every move? Catching all my words, facial expressions, actions, and reactions on camera. And then what if someone packaged it all together and played it on some sort of reality TV show for all the world to see? What would be the glaring message of my life?

I'm convicted thinking about this.

You see, if someone were to ask me, "What are you all about?" I would have some nice-sounding answers. But what actually happens during the strains of everyday life can sometimes betray my best intentions.

I want to be a loving mom. But my family seems to know the exact buttons to push that send me into a tailspin of emotion and exhaustion.

I want to be a strong witness for Christ. So why is it I can read my Bible first thing in the morning and then find myself honking at the person who cuts me off in traffic just an hour later?

I realize there is a place for God's tender mercies for me in all this. But I also know that while no TV cameras are following me around, my life is speaking a message about what I really believe, and I want that message to honor Jesus.

> *My life is speaking a message about what I really believe, and I want that message to honor Jesus.*

I once heard, "Great sermons are not preached, they are lived." Oh how I long to live a message that speaks loud and clear, "Jesus is true and the principles found in His teachings work!"

Let's just be honest: It's tough being a sold-out soul for Christ stuck in a body that's so tempted to sin. That's why it's essential that I view my time with God each morning as a preparation and an invitation.

- *Preparation:* Our key verse reminds us, "All Scripture is God-breathed and is useful for teaching, rebuking, correcting and training in righteousness, so that the servant of God may be thoroughly equipped for every good work" (2 Timothy 3:16–17).

Every verse I read is part of God's preparation for me that day. So, instead of just rushing to check off my to-do list that I spent a few minutes with God, I must allow His teachings to seep into my heart and mind. Then I can prayerfully ask God to interrupt my natural flesh response and remind me throughout the day of the truths He taught me that morning.

- *Invitation:* The next essential view of my quiet time each morning is recognizing I've just invited Jesus to do life with me, so I need to look for His activity throughout my day. My minute-by-minute theme becomes, *"Not my will, God, but Yours be done."*

So if something happens that causes my flesh to want to rear up and act ugly, I can say, *"Not my will, God, but Yours be done."* This slight pause and acknowledgment of God redirects my frustration and replaces it with grace. And most wonderful of all, it helps me connect my time with Jesus to everyday life choices. Making that connection is one of the ways we personally hear from and experience God.

I know sometimes it's hard to spend time with Jesus first thing in the morning. And I'm certainly not trying to make this just another demand on our time. But Jesus' invitation to us to sit with Him is such an incredible gift. He loves us so much He wants to help us. He knows what each day holds, and He longs to prepare us for every single thing He sees coming our way.

Let's accept His invitation to sit with Him. Let's listen to Him intently. And let's ask Him to intervene before our natural reactions to things betray our best intentions. Then we will be able to live lives that speak to the fact that we have spent time with Jesus . . . and without saying a word, our imperfect lives will be a God-honoring sermon.

Dear Lord, please teach me how to reveal more and more of You through the way I live my life. I want to tell the whole world about You using words only when necessary. In Jesus' Name, Amen.

5

IS THIS THE RIGHT DECISION?

This is my prayer: that your love may abound more
and more in knowledge and depth of insight, so
that you may be able to discern what is best and may
be pure and blameless for the day of Christ.
—PHILIPPIANS 1:9–10

Have you ever had that deep-down knowing of what to do in a situation but ignored it? I understand.

I was home alone recently when a large box was delivered to my doorstep.

The delivery man graciously brought it inside. But I figured it might be a bit much for me to ask him to take it past the foyer, up the stairs, and down the hall.

So there it sat, this mysterious, heavy box.

Deep inside, I knew this was nothing but some product one of my people had ordered.

But I didn't listen to that internal awareness. I ignored it and listened to my fears instead. You know you've watched one too many mystery TV shows when your first thought about a mysterious box sitting in your foyer is that a person with scary intentions could fit inside. Yes, a crazy person with weapons could mail himself right into your foyer and sit there all day, quietly waiting until you went to bed.

So I kicked the side of the box to see if there was any kind of reflex action from a living thing inside of it. There wasn't, of course. But then I decided, just to be sure, I would stand around the corner from the box to see if I could step out of its line of sight and possibly hear something: a cough, a sneeze—anything.

I could leave no room for doubts, no room at all for any possible bad outcome from this box—a box that I eventually opened with a knife. Just in case. Only to discover a dorm-room refrigerator that someone had ordered.

I wasted half my day worrying about a box that contained a dorm fridge.

Find that courageous yes. Fight for that confident no.

But we do this sometimes. We have a decision to make and we have that deep-down knowing. We know what to do. We know what the answer is. But we don't go with that knowing. We overprocess the what-ifs and the maybes until we find ourselves standing around a corner listening to see if a cardboard box containing a refrigerator might sneeze.

Now, there are certainly some decisions that need to be processed. But then there are other decisions we just simply need to say yes or no to and move on.

Find that courageous yes. Fight for that confident no. Know it. State it. Own it.

Sometimes it just comes down to that deep whisper within that says, "Uh-huh, yes." Or a simple, "No, not that."

God has woven into us the ability to discern what is best if we're closely following Him. Let's read our key verse again: "This is my prayer: that your love may abound more and more in knowledge and depth of insight, so that you may be able to discern *what is best* and may be pure and blameless for the day of Christ" (Philippians 1:9–10, emphasis mine).

As we layer knowledge and depth of insight into our lives, we develop a trustworthy discernment.

Knowledge is wisdom that comes from acquiring truth.

Insight is wisdom that comes from living out the truth we acquire.

Discernment is wisdom that comes from the Holy Spirit's reminders of that knowledge and insight.

I know a young mom who has really been struggling with the decision of whether to let her two-year-old go to preschool a couple of half days a week next year. As I listened to her, I felt compelled to ask her three questions:

1. Have you been reading and praying through God's Word?
2. Have you been applying God's Word to your mothering?
3. Have you sought godly counsel and insights from wise people who know specifics about your situation?

The answer to all three of those simple questions was yes, so I reminded her that God had assigned her to be this child's mother. If she had done these three things, then she had the ability to discern what was best.

She didn't need to wait for some big neon sign to drop down from heaven to know what to do. If she had that deep knowing that this was a no answer for her child, then she should go with that. If she had that deep knowing that this was a yes answer for her child, then she should go with that.

It's not about trusting ourselves. Rather, it's about trusting the Holy Spirit to do what Jesus promised us in John 14:26: "The Advocate, the Holy Spirit, whom the Father will send in my name, will teach you all things and will remind you of everything I have said to you."

When we've done what we need to do to acquire the knowledge and insight of truth, then the discernment of that truth is there. We must learn to trust and use that discernment because the more we do this, the more wisdom we acquire to make God-honoring decisions.

Dear Lord, I want to make decisions that honor You. Lead me as I develop a trustworthy discernment. In Jesus' Name, Amen.

6

AN AGENDA THAT WILL NEVER SATISFY

He appointed twelve that they might be with
him and that he might send them out to preach
and to have authority to drive out demons.

—MARK 3:14–15

I should have been happy. I knew it. I could have listed so many things for which I was thankful.

So, what was this undercurrent of disappointment that ebbed and flowed just beneath the surface of my more honest moments? I got still and I got sad.

I was doing a lot, pouring myself out for God, but not really spending time getting refilled by God.

Maybe you can relate?

We run at a breakneck pace to try and achieve what God wants us to slow down enough to receive.

He really does have it all worked out. The gaps filled. The needs met. The questions answered. The problems solved.

And the parts He's purposed for us? They're all perfectly portioned out in assignments meant for us today. No more. No less.

All He asks is that we personally receive from Him before setting out to work for Him. In doing so we are fueled by His power and encouraged by His presence. This is the daily sacred exchange where ministry duty turns into pure delight.

How it must break His heart when we work like we don't believe He's capable. We say we trust Him but act like everything depends on us. We give all we have to the tasks at hand with only occasional leftovers of time to slightly acknowledge Him.

Imagine a little girl running while holding a cup, sloshing out all it contains. She thinks what will refill her is just ahead. So she presses on with sheer determination, clutching an empty cup.

She keeps running toward an agenda He never set, one that will never satisfy.

She sees Him and holds out her cup. But she catches only a few drops as she runs by Him because she didn't stop long enough to be filled up. Empty can't be tempered with mere drops.

> *We run at a breakneck pace to try and achieve what God wants us to slow down enough to receive.*

The tragic truth is what will fill her . . . what will fill us . . . isn't the accomplishment just ahead.

That shiny thing is actually a vacuum that sucks us dry—but never has the ability to refill.

I should know, because that's where I was. There's no kind of empty quite like this empty—where your hands are full but inside you're nothing but an exhausted shell.

I knew it would take slow moments to get me out of this empty place.

I needed to reconnect with the One who knows how to breathe

life back into depleted and dead places. Jesus doesn't participate in the rat race. He's into the slower rhythms of life like abiding, delighting, and dwelling—all words used to describe us being with Him.

As a matter of fact, when Jesus appointed the disciples, there were two parts to their calling, as we see in Mark 3:14–15.

Yes, they were to go to preach and drive out demons, but the first part of their calling was to "be with him."

Fullness comes when we remember to *be with Him* before going out to serve Him.

He wants our hearts in alignment with Him before our hands set about doing today's assignment for Him.

So, He extends what we need and invites us each day to receive in prayer, worship, and truth from His Word. And He lovingly replenishes our cup while whispering: "This isn't a race to test the fastest pace. I just want you to persevere on the path I have marked out especially for you. Fix your eyes, not on a worldly prize, but on staying in love with Me."

That's an agenda that's always completely satisfying.

Dear Lord, I'm choosing to stop in the midst of everything to just be with You. Let me never forget what a gift it is to spend this sacred time in Your presence. In Jesus' Name, Amen.

PREPARING FOR ADVENTURE

Open my eyes that I may see wonderful things in your law.
—PSALM 119:18

*O*h, how we underestimate the power made available to us when we spend time with God. Our earthly eyes are so limited because they don't allow us to see what is happening in the heavenly realm. A daily battle is being fought for our attention and our devotion. Satan would love nothing more than to keep us separated from the power God gives us during our time with Him. It's time to stop feeling guilty and ill-equipped and start embracing the incredible privilege of meeting with Jesus every day.

Remember, this time doesn't have to be perfect to be powerful and effective. Jesus just wants a willing soul to come to Him—to verbalize her desire to seek Him and acknowledge her need for Him. Then He'll show her how to make each moment with Him exactly what she needs.

Satan would love to keep us separated from the power God gives us during our time with Him.

Most days before I start my time with the Lord, I pray a very simple prayer that ushers my heart into the right place with God:

God, I want to see You. God, I want to hear You. God, I want to know You. So that I can follow hard after You.

This prayer is not a magic formula, just four short sentences that perfectly express my desire to experience God throughout my day. I want to see Him working in me, around me, and through me. I want to hear His voice so clearly that I won't doubt when He asks for my obedience. I want to know Him—not just facts about Him—but really know Him personally and intimately. And lastly, I want to follow hard after Him, to be the woman He wants me to be in every circumstance of my day.

It's amazing that when I verbalize my heart's desire in this way, something inside me shifts and I'm ready for the Word of God in a fresh way. It reminds me of the psalmist's request in Psalm 119:18: "Open my eyes that I may see wonderful things in your law." A request God delights in answering.

I don't want to just read and pray to check it off my to-do list. I see this time, instead, as preparation for the great adventure God and I are about to head off on together in the hours ahead. Now what could be more exciting than that?

Dear Lord, I want to see You. I want to hear You. I want to know You. Please help me recognize Your presence in my day today so that I can follow hard after You. In Jesus' Name, Amen.

8

INTERRUPTED BY JESUS

"Blessed are the pure in heart,
for they will see God."
—MATTHEW 5:8

When we connect with Jesus and see Him, we will be changed. Changed in the best kind of way. Jesus will be so real that we won't be able to be anything but completely devoted to Him.

I can hardly go through anything in life without seeing God's hand in it. Layer upon layer of these constant experiences with God have built a very secure foundation of faith.

This raises a few concerns. Am I overspiritualizing my life? What if I don't have these experiences, or what if an experience I attribute to God isn't from Him at all? I understand these questions. I remember being skeptical. Part of me wanted something deeper with God, but I was scared.

A larger part of me wanted God to be explainable and safe. Fitting Him in a box ensured that I ran no risk of being interrupted by Him. I just wanted to do my part (be good) and have Him do His (bless me). It was a comfortable arrangement. But it was also the very perspective that numbed my spirit and rendered my faith ineffective.

I remember hearing my Bible friends talking freely about hearing from God and seeing Him in remarkable ways. I called them my "Bible friends" while my eyes rolled and my voice mocked their enthusiasm.

Finally God got a hold of me while I was reading Henry Blackaby's book *Experiencing God,* in which he encourages us to look for God's activity all around us. There was not even a hint of doubt in Blackaby's statements. He was absolutely certain that if we desired to see God, we would.

Paul writes to the Corinthian church, "It is written: 'What no eye has seen, and what no ear has heard, and what no human mind has conceived'—the things God has pre-pared for those who love him—*these are the things God has revealed to us by his Spirit.* The Spirit searches all things, even the deep things of God" (1 Corinthians 2:9–10, emphasis mine).

It is possible for God's Spirit to reveal to us the deep things of God.

If we have accepted Christ as our Savior, we have God's Spirit in us. Therefore, it is possible for God's Spirit to reveal to us the deep things of God.

How does this happen most often? In the midst of everyday life using everyday things. Divine mixed in our mundane. It's the stuff all Jesus' parables were made of.

So what do you do if you aren't currently experiencing God in this way? The Bible tells us that those with a pure heart will see God (Matthew 5:8). It doesn't say we have to be perfect or perfectly ready; it just says that we have to get to a place where our hearts purely desire to see Him—and then we will.

Tell God of your desires. Ask Him to reveal anything that may be blocking your view. And then start looking. Seeing God changes us, grows us, and strengthens us to become more than people with mere knowledge of God. We become changed people who live out the reality of God.

> *Dear Lord, I want to see Your hand and hear Your voice in my life. Please show me if there are things that block my view of You, so I can deal with them. I want to see You and be changed by You. In Jesus' Name, Amen.*

9

IF YOU'RE FEELING OVERLOOKED AND UNAPPRECIATED . . .

> The LORD said to Samuel, "Do not consider his outward
> appearance or his height, for I have rejected him. The LORD
> does not look at the things people look at. People look at
> the outward appearance, but the LORD looks at the heart."
> —1 SAMUEL 16:7

Sometimes I wake up in the morning feeling a little grumpy. *Time to do it all again.* I'll buy food that gets eaten. I'll wash clothes that get dirty again. I'll sweep floors that will somehow need to be swept again before the day is even done.

Is there more to all this than just doing the tasks of everyday life?

One day before I jumped into the normal routine, I sat with Jesus. And I found some big truths as I read my Bible and took a little glance into David's life. Despite how others saw him, his own tendency to sin, and lack of position in his own family, David had the sweet reassurance of God. And that was enough.

Overlooked by everyone else. Handpicked by God.

To his older brothers, David was young . . . possibly even a pest. To his father, Jesse, he was just another son. To onlookers, he was a mere shepherd boy. But to God, David was the one destined to be king of Israel. And not just any king. He was from the bloodline from which Jesus would come.

Overlooked by everyone else. Handpicked by God.

Even the way David was anointed to be the future king is a telling story. In 1 Samuel 16, God reveals to Samuel that He has rejected Saul as king and chosen one of Jesse's sons to be the replacement.

Think of the list of qualifications that must have run through Samuel's mind for such a position: tall, smart, articulate, brave, groomed, well-mannered, a natural-born leader. Samuel saw some of these characteristics in Eliab, David's brother. "The LORD said to Samuel, 'Do not consider his outward appearance or his height, for I have rejected him. The LORD does not look at the things people look at. People look at the outward appearance, but the LORD looks at the heart'" (1 Samuel 16:7).

> *Overlooked by everyone else. Handpicked by God.*

Samuel had Jesse line up all of his sons before him. All of them were to be considered. Yet, Jesse didn't call David in from tending sheep. Was this an oversight? An assumption? A judgment call? A deliberate choice?

Overlooked by everyone else. Handpicked by God.

Samuel passes on each of Jesse's sons and then asks, "Are these all the sons you have?" I imagine Jesse with a quizzical expression replying, "There is still the youngest . . . He is tending the sheep" (1 Samuel 16:11). Surely one who spends his time taking care of animals is not the one to take care of a nation.

Overlooked by everyone else. Handpicked by God.

As soon as Samuel saw David, he knew he'd found the one. David was anointed to become king. But he was not immediately ushered to the throne. It would be many years before David was recognized by the world. So, where did he go after being anointed as king? To a refining school? A government academy? Military training? Nope.

He went back out to the fields and continued to shepherd his flock. A king-to-be doing lowly tasks. A future king whose character was refined in the fields of everyday life to prepare him for his calling.

How like us. In the midst of smelly laundry, dirty dishes, snotty noses, misplaced keys, overdue library books, bills, and that birthday gift that still needs to be mailed—there is training. There is character building. There is attitude shaping. There is soul defining. All of which must take place for us to become what God intends.

Do you ever feel overlooked by the world? Take heart—we are handpicked by God.

We aren't just doing tasks. We are building a legacy. We are shaping God's Kingdom. We are in the process of not only discovering our calling but that of our family as well. And I don't know about you, but it sure does make me look at my everyday tasks (yes, even the smelly laundry) in a whole different light.

Dear Lord, I'm grateful that even when I feel overlooked,
I can rest in the fact that I am handpicked by You. Help me
live my life for an audience of One. In Jesus' Name, Amen.

10

I'M SCARED TO PRAY BOLDLY

The prayer of a righteous person is powerful and effective.
—JAMES 5:16

ometimes I'm scared to pray boldly.

It's not at all that I don't believe God can do anything. I absolutely do. I'm a wild-about-Jesus girl. Wild in my willingness. Wild in my obedience. Wild in my adventures with God.

So my hesitation isn't rooted in any kind of doubt about God. It's more rooted in doubts about myself and my ability to absolutely discern the will of God. The reality is, sometimes God chooses not to do things. And if His will is "No," while I am boldly praying for a "Yes," it makes me feel out of step with God.

Can you relate?

I so desperately want to stay in the will of God that I find myself praying with clauses like: *God, please heal my friend, but if it's Your will to take her, I will trust You.*

I wonder why I don't just boldly pray: *God, please heal my friend.* And then stand confidently knowing my prayers were not in vain—no matter what the outcome.

Praying boldly boots me out of that stale place of religious habit into authentic connection with God Himself.

Prayer opens my spiritual eyes to see things I can't see on my own. And I'm convinced prayer matters. Prayers are powerful and effective if prayed from the position of a righteous heart (James 5:16).

Prayer opens my spiritual eyes to see things I can't see on my own.

So, prayer does make a difference—a life-changing, mind-blowing, earth-rattling difference. We don't need to know how. We don't need to know when. We just need to kneel confidently and know the tremors of a simple Jesus girl's prayers extend far-wide and far-high and far-deep.

Letting that absolute truth slosh over into my soul snuffs out the flickers of hesitation. It bends my stiff knees. And it ignites a fresh, bold, and even wilder fire within. Not bold as in bossy and demanding. But bold as in, *I love my Jesus with all my heart, so why would I offer anything less than an ignited prayer life?*

Jesus speaks specifically about igniting our prayer lives in Matthew 6, verses 6–8: "When you pray, go into your room, close the door and pray to your Father, who is unseen. Then your Father, who sees what is done in secret, will reward you. And when you pray, do not keep on babbling like pagans, for they think they will be heard because of their many words. Do not be like them, for your Father knows what you need before you ask him."

So let's ask. And ask again. Not because we can cause God to move, but so we'll position our souls to see our sweet Jesus move in any which way He pleases.

Dear Lord, I'm so grateful for the opportunity to bring all my worries and cares to You. Thank You for providing me with exactly what I need. I trust You have my best interest in mind today. In Jesus' Name, Amen.

11

FOLLOW ME

Trust in the LORD with all your heart
    and lean not on your own understanding;
in all your ways submit to him,
    and he will make your paths straight.

—PROVERBS 3:5–6

Many years ago, I was an attendee at a conference. It was a business conference, but the Christian leadership made it seem more like a revival than a meeting. A number of the speakers challenged us to pursue God like never before.

After one of the sessions I beelined it to the bathroom where a long line had already formed. When I finally reached an open stall, I realized the woman before me had left her conference notebook behind.

Not finding the owner in the bathroom, I flipped open the binder to see if a name was written inside, and the first handwriting I saw was the words "ministry to women." At the risk of being totally nosy, I kept reading. Basically the owner of the notebook had written that this would be the year she would finally get intentional about pursuing the ministry to women God had placed on her heart.

As I read those words, I felt Jesus' invitation, "Follow Me," and didn't hesitate to say yes. You see, in my journey to live completely with God every day, I have learned the treasure of expectation. As we've talked about in previous devotions, I ask God to help me live in expectation of experiencing Him; therefore, I do. It's not that I go around getting involved in every situation around me. But I do ask God to

The more we follow Jesus, the more we fall in love with Him.

make me wise and aware of which opportunities are mine. This day, I knew exactly how to follow Jesus completely in this situation.

At the risk of having this woman think I was crazy, I wrote off to the side of her notes, "I might be able to help you with this. Call me if you'd like. Lysa TerKeurst with Proverbs 31 Ministries." I added my cell phone number and got the notebook to Lost and Found at the information desk.

Days went by, the conference ended, and almost a week later, I'd forgotten about the whole thing. And then the call came.

From the start of my conversation with Tracey, I could tell that God Himself had arranged this divine encounter. To make a long story short, my simple note was the confirmation from God for which she'd been fervently praying. Tracey and I were both blown away. Later, she sent me a note that said in part, "Just within the past week, after speaking with you, God has begun to open up doors like you would not believe. (Well, I guess you would!) Thank you for your obedience in writing the note and for being such an inspiration!"

My encounter with Tracey was yet another reminder that the more we follow Jesus, the more we fall in love with Him, want to obey Him, experience life with Him, and become a beacon of light to others through Him. It was also a reminder to keep on living out the command we find in our key verse: "Trust in the LORD with all your heart and lean not on your own understanding; in all your ways submit to him, and he will make your paths straight" (Proverbs 3:5–6).

Do you feel a tug at your heart to live completely with God, but you are still uncertain about pursuing it? Why not ask God to reveal Himself to you in the coming days and confirm exactly what He has for you? The adventure that follows just might blow you away.

Will it be inconvenient? Maybe.

Will it cost you in ways that stretch you? Sometimes.

Does it force you to live life with a less self-centered outlook? Yes.

Does living to follow Jesus at every turn bring joy that you can't get any other way? Absolutely.

It is the very thing your soul was created to do. It is the most daily way to discover your purpose in life.

Dear Lord, I want to know You, experience You, follow You, and obey You. Please reveal Yourself to me. Please show me how You want me to follow You. In Jesus' Name, Amen.

12

HEARING GOD'S INVITATIONS

*Whether you turn to the right or to the left, your ears will
hear a voice behind you, saying, "This is the way; walk in it."*
—ISAIAH 30:21

I have to admit, I rush and miss God's invitations a lot. I walked by a woman at church the other day with pale skin and a bald head. A quick stirring in my heart said, *Go say hi.* I brushed it off.

I saw a discarded cup in the parking lot of the restaurant where I had lunch. I knew I was supposed to pick it up and throw it away. I walked right by it.

These were simple acts of obedience I missed. But not missed because I was unaware. They were missed because I was busy—caught in the rush of endless demands. And the rush makes us rebellious. I knew what to do and blatantly ignored it.

Ignoring God's leading doesn't seem like such a big deal in these cases. In the grand scheme of the world, how big a thing is it that I didn't pick up that cup? After all, how can I be sure it was really God?

I think a better question would be, *How can I be sure it wasn't God?*

As God's girls, we long for unbroken companionship with Him. The cup was a little deal unless it was me breaking away from obeying His instruction. The one who obeys God's instruction for today will develop a keen awareness of His direction for tomorrow. I'm always

- 35 -

asking God for direction, but I'll miss it if I constantly ignore His instruction.

It's in those little breaks in our companionship with God where confusion sets in about what we're really supposed to do.

Have you ever heard that amazing verse from Isaiah that says, "Whether you turn to the right or to the left, your ears will hear a voice behind you, saying, 'This is the way; walk in it'" (30:21)?

I love this verse! I want it to be true for me! I want my ears to hear God say, "This is the way; walk in it."

I want that with every fiber of my being. And when I humbly repented for rushing past the opportunities God had given me, He graciously gave me a do-over.

The one who obeys God's instruction for today will develop a keen awareness of His direction for tomorrow.

I remembered the woman I hurried by at church. I felt a stirring to track her down through a mutual friend and send a simple email. Just a small note. Which I sent. For no other reason than God saying, "This touch is one of your assignments for today. Don't miss it."

That email paved the road for me to have coffee with this woman. During that coffee, God gave me an answer to something I'd been begging Him to speak to me about. I thought I was going to help her and I was the one helped. Obeying God's instruction led to me being able to discern His direction. I needed that coffee meeting, and it never would have happened had I not stopped the rush of my life and sent the email to the woman God had prompted me to connect with.

That little act of obedience somehow unplugged my spiritual ears. Not that we can't hear God otherwise. But hearing Him clearly? I think that might require my soul to acknowledge what all my rushing causes me to miss.

Yes, if we want His direction for our decisions, the great longings of our souls must not only be the big moments of assignment. They must also be the seemingly small instructions in the most ordinary of moments when God points His Spirit finger saying, *Go there.* And in doing that, we are companions of God with eyes and ears more open, more able, more in tune with Him.

Dear Lord, I confess that I do walk right past Your
invitations sometimes. Please forgive me for those times
I have rushed right on by. Help me to stop and follow
You. I'm listening. In Jesus' Name, Amen.

13

A LIFE WITH EXTRAORDINARY IMPACT

After Ehud came Shamgar son of Anath, who struck down
six hundred Philistines with an oxgoad. He too saved Israel.
—JUDGES 3:31

I am a woman who wants to make a difference for Christ in the world. I want my life and legacy to count for something with eternal significance. I want to stand before God one day knowing I fulfilled the purposes He had for me.

But there's always this nagging sense inside me that the world's problems are too big, and I'm too small.

Can you relate? That's why I'm so fascinated with Shamgar.

We learn who Shamgar is in one small verse hiding at the very end of the third chapter of Judges: "After Ehud came Shamgar son of Anath, who struck down six hundred Philistines with an oxgoad. He too saved Israel" (Judges 3:31).

Tucked into this one verse, we see three things Shamgar did that resulted in his life having extraordinary impact:

1. He offered God his willingness.
2. He used what God had given him.
3. He stayed true to who he was.

And in doing those three things, it was enough. God used him to save the nation of Israel.

Oh, how Shamgar's story stirs my soul. He was an ordinary person, in an ordinary place, doing an ordinary job. The thing that made him extraordinary wasn't anything external. It was his internal drive to do the right thing and be obedient to God, right where he was. His job was to be obedient to God. God's job was everything else.

The same is possible for us. If we are obedient to God in the midst of our ordinary lives, extraordinary impact is always possible.

I doubt Shamgar ever expected to be used by God to save the nation of Israel. When we take a closer look at his life, we see several things that could have left him feeling like the wrong man for a "Deliverer of Israel" job title.

First is the matter of his background. "Shamgar" is a name with Canaanite roots, not Hebrew. This fact has led some scholars to believe it's entirely possible Shamgar was both Jew and Gentile. And since God had commanded His people not to intermarry with Gentiles, Shamgar's lack of a pure bloodline from his parents could have easily led him to label himself an unlikely candidate for a mighty work of God.

Then there is the matter of his occupation. Shamgar's use of an oxgoad (another word for a cattle prod) to kill the Philistines implies he may have been a farmer. Can we just stop and process that for a moment?

He was a farmer. Up against an organized army. Of six hundred men. If I had been Shamgar, I imagine I'd have been raising my hand with a few questions for the Lord. Questions like, "Are You positive You've got the right person?"

If we are obedient to God in the midst of our ordinary lives, extraordinary impact is always possible.

And we can't skim over Shamgar's choice of weapon. Talk about unlikely and ordinary. An oxgoad was typically used to prod oxen, not wage war. But since the Philistines would not allow the Israelites to have any weapons (1 Samuel 13:19–22), they were forced to use whatever they had on hand. So Shamgar simply sharpened what he had and offered it to the Lord.

I love that God's hand is never limited by what we have in ours.

Do you long to live a life that has extraordinary impact? I pray you will grab hold of the encouragement found in Shamgar's story.

Offer God your willingness. Even if you feel small . . . even if you feel unlikely . . . even if everything in you is screaming you're not someone who can be used by God . . . simply offer Him your willingness.

Use what God has given you. What's in your hand, sweet friend? What gift, what talent, what ability? Whatever it is, take time to sharpen it. And choose to believe God can use it when you humbly offer it up to Him.

Stay true to who you are. God didn't ask Shamgar to be anyone other than a farmer. He's not asking you to be anyone other than who He designed you to be, either. You do you, and then watch with humble amazement as God uses your willing, obedient, ordinary life to accomplish extraordinary things in His name.

Lord, thank You for reminding me that You can use anyone and everyone. I willingly offer You all that I am and all that I have—choosing to believe that who I am is enough to be used by You. In Jesus' Name, Amen.

14

YOUR UNIQUE CALLING

*We are God's handiwork, created in Christ Jesus to do
good works, which God prepared in advance for us to do.*
—Ephesians 2:10

had wanted a red coat for years. But paying full price for a coat seemed excessive when I had several perfectly fine coats in my closet. So, each year I decided to wait until coats went on clearance and then I'd treat myself.

But every year, by the time the coats went on clearance, the weather flip-flopped. Who wants to spend their clothing budget on a red coat when just the thought of walking outside makes you sweat?

At last, one winter, I happened upon a discount clothing store that was having a clearance sale. In the window was a red coat. On sale! While it was still cold outside!

I wanted to get the coat right then. However, I had a store coupon for an additional 50 percent off that wasn't good until a week later. That would make the coat a most fabulous deal. So I hung my treasure back on the rack, determined to return and get it the following week.

A few days later, I was out and about again when I got a call that several of my bed comforters were ready for pick up at the local laundromat.

When I arrived to gather them up, I saw a woman with two young children, all wearing threadbare clothing. I made small talk with the kids about what a fun time of year Christmas is; they looked away and didn't say a word. Out of the corner of my eye, I saw their mom hang her head. I wished them a Merry Christmas and scurried out.

As soon as I started to drive off, God pricked my heart. "You looked at those kids, but chose not to really see them. Go back. Help them. Help her."

But I didn't have any cash. How could I help? What would she think of me? Would I offend her by giving her a check? I didn't even know her name to write on a check.

I put the car in park, pulled out my checkbook, and suddenly I knew the exact amount I was to give her. The full price of that red coat.

You were created to participate in God's divine activity.

I walked back into the laundromat and handed her the check. "You'll just need to write your name on this, and I promise my bank will cash it. It's not much, but I'd love for you to take it and buy your kids something fun for Christmas."

Shocked, she thanked me. As I turned to leave, she called out her name, the name God has engraved on the palm of His hand, the one He loves and hears and cares so deeply about.

Funny enough, I went into the red coat store the next day to return some pants. Every one of those red coats I'd wanted so much was gone. So I bought a red scarf on clearance instead and smiled, for in that moment, I knew I'd fulfilled my calling for this page of my life.

Oh, sweet friend, you have a calling, a unique and wondrous calling from God every day of your life. Truth we find spelled out clearly in Ephesians 2:10: "We are God's handiwork, created in Christ Jesus to do good works, which God prepared in advance for us to do." Today it could be in your local laundromat; tomorrow it could be a phone conversation with a friend. Wherever it is, whatever it is, remember: you were created to participate in God's divine activity.

Lord, I want to love the ones whose names are engraved upon Your hands. Help me to really see others and their needs as I journey along this path You've called me to. In Jesus' Name, Amen.

15

REST AND REASSURANCE

"Come to me, all you who are weary and
burdened, and I will give you rest."
—MATTHEW 11:28

We all have those times we wish the voice of God would audibly speak so loudly there's no way we could miss it: "This is the direction I want you to go." Then we'd know whether to stay the course or head in a new direction.

Have you ever wished for this kind of certainty?

I have.

Most of us want to know what to do. Without that confidence, sometimes we stay in a place too long. But the greater loss happens in those times we quit too soon. Then, we can live with this nagging sense of "what if?" What if I'd persevered one more year, one more month, one more day?

Knowing when to stop and when to keep on keeping on is a cru-cial life lesson. One I want to learn well. Often, the more I struggle on my own, the less confident I am with the right next step. It's exhausting!

I must do all I can do. Then trust God will do what only He can do.

But the truth is, I don't need to be confused or tired. There is one central place I can go for direction and rest. In Matthew 11:28 Jesus encourages us, "Come to me, all you who are weary and burdened, and I will give you rest."

I used to get so frustrated with this verse because I thought, *I don't want rest. I want reassurance! I'm burdened by this decision I have to make. I don't want to mess up by missing a cue from You, God.*

But the rest Jesus offers is not a spiritual sleep aid. The Greek word for this kind of rest is *anapauo*, which has as one of its definitions, "of calm and patient expectation."

In other words, Jesus is saying, *If you come to Me, I will take your exhaustion and uncertainty and turn it into a calm expectation.*

But how?

My friend Jennifer Rothschild does this enlightening exercise at some of her conferences. She tells the audience to imagine her writing two different words on a large chalkboard. She then speaks the letters as she draws the first word into the air . . . R-E-S-T. She does the same for the second word . . . R-E-S-I-S-T. Then she asks what is the difference?

The difference is, of course, "I."

"I don't know what to do." "I can't figure this out." "I'm worn out." "I've tried everything I know to do." "I've given all I have to give."

I'm familiar with these "I" statements because I've said them myself.

We can only find *anapauo* rest—fresh hope—as we stop running ragged and simply take on the next assignment Jesus gives.

In verse 29 of Matthew 11, Jesus gives us the assignment: to take on His yoke and learn from Him. Ask Jesus to show you how to rest in Him. It might mean sitting quietly, asking others to join you in prayer, or clearing your calendar to read the Word. Once you're still, take the next step. Not ten steps. Not the whole path. Not the Google map with the highlighted route. Just the next step. You'll know it because it'll be in line with God's character and His Word.

Complete that step with excellence and an open, humble heart. Listen and look for all Jesus wants to teach you in this next step.

This is your part of the equation.

But after the assignment comes the reassurance in verse 30, "My yoke is easy and my burden is light." We don't have to have all the answers. We just have to stay connected to the One who does. Where our strength ends is the exact point where His will begins.

This is God's part of the equation.

I must do all I can do. Then trust God will do what only He can do.

Should I stay? Should I go? Maybe the better question is, "God, what is the next step I'm to take today? I'm going to do my part. And trust the rest to You."

Dear Lord, I am tired, and I can't figure things out. Please help me see Your part in this equation. Where my strength ends is where Your will begins. Help me, Lord, to look to You for my very next step. I will wait in calm expectation. In Jesus' Name, Amen.

16

SPACE TO EXHALE

"If you keep your feet from breaking the Sabbath and from doing as you please on my holy day, if you call the Sabbath a delight and the LORD's holy day honorable, and if you honor it by not going your own way and not doing as you please or speaking idle words, then you will find your joy in the LORD."

—ISAIAH 58:13–14

*R*est.

That sounds so good, but it's really difficult for a girl like me. Even when my physical body is at rest, my mind rarely is.

I feel like I'm always juggling balls in my brain. My family's needs. Home demands. Work projects. The to-do lists never stop.

Yet the Bible makes it very clear that we are to honor the Sabbath day and pursue rest. Literally we are to hit the pause button on life once a week and guard our need to rest. Guard it fiercely. Guard it intentionally. Guard it even if our schedules beg us to do otherwise.

But why?

There are honest, personal reasons we need to observe the Sabbath that will be unique for each person. There are private conversations we need to have with God. We all need to pause, to sit with God, and ask Him to reveal some things to us.

We read in Isaiah 58:13–14, "If you keep your feet from breaking the Sabbath and from doing as you please on my holy day, if you call the Sabbath a delight and the LORD's holy day honorable, and if you honor it by not going your own way and not doing as you please or speaking idle words, then you will find your joy in the LORD."

When I consider these words, something occurs to me—it's not just a day for me to give to God. It's a day God established for me. He wants to give me something if only I'll slow down enough to receive it.

The Sabbath isn't merely a time to be observed; it's a time to be preserved. It's a time to rediscover our joy in the Lord.

I need this. I want to be a preserver of this day—one who is determined to protect this day of personal preservation and rediscover the delight of God.

The Sabbath isn't merely a time to be observed; it's a time to be preserved.

The observer remembers to rest.

The preserver rests to remember—to remember that it's all about God.

The observer remembers to rest and pause on the Sabbath day in order to follow a rule.

The preserver does more than follow a rule. She follows God's desire and embraces His purpose in the rest. She spends one day a week letting the fresh wind of God's rest blow through her, cleaning out all she's been taking in during the week with a purifying soul exhale.

It's all about pausing and connecting with God without the distracting chaos of our everyday routines. For one day a week, we step out of the fray and let God direct our day according to His rhythm, not ours.

God's rhythm preserves a space in us to hear His voice, reveals the places we're off track, and prevents us from being filled with unnecessary clutter. Quiet rest allows us to see the places where we're going our own way, the areas where we're more self-pleasing than God-pleasing, the idle words that need to be reined in. During the downtime, we can deal with the mental clutter and focus on the ways of God.

The Sabbath makes this possible.

Taking one day for rest gives my soul the freedom it so desperately needs. Freedom to breathe. Space to breathe. Inhaling and exhaling in a gentle rhythm set by God.

Dear Lord, space to breathe—this is what I need today.
Thank You for showing me how important it is to create
a place for freedom and rest. In Jesus' Name. Amen.

17

CHASING DOWN OUR DECISIONS

The prudent see danger and take refuge,
but the simple keep going and pay the penalty.
—PROVERBS 27:12

One of the best things that happened in my early twenties was that the guy I thought I was going to marry broke my heart. That devastation at first sent me to bed wallowing in a fit of despair and depression. Then it sent me looking for new possibilities to ease the ache of his absence in the bars my coworkers would frequent after work.

One weekend I hit such a low, I refused to get out of bed. After I had hidden for several days in that dark apartment bedroom, my roommate came in and announced I needed two things. She yanked the blinds open and said the first was a little light. Then she held up a newspaper ad for a large church in town. Her second suggestion was clear. In her quirky, Southern drawl, she quipped, "Now this is where you need to be meeting people. Not at them bars you've been going to."

I love that girl for teaching me something profound that day. I needed light. Both in the physical sense and in the spiritual sense. But even more than that I needed a new direction. A direction that would take me where I really wanted to go. Since I didn't understand that quite yet, I only listened half-heartedly and tucked the newspaper ad between my bed and nightstand.

The next day I gathered myself up just enough to drag myself into work. After work, several of the guys were heading to the bar down the street. I needed some fun, I reasoned, so off I went.

A couple of hours later we were playing pool and drinking. One of the guys offered to make me a late dinner back at his place. I honestly wanted to go. I was lonely. I was miserable. I was hungry. But I pictured my roommate holding up that ad for church and something wrestled my heart into declining his offer.

Had I gone on that date with the guy from the bar, it would have set my vulnerable heart on a vulnerable path. I don't want to presume I know where it would have taken me. But I do know it wouldn't have taken me closer to the truth I needed.

That next night after work, I pulled the ad out and scanned it. The next Sunday I went to that church.

Now, I'm not saying the act of going to church fixes everything. Just as simply looking at a restaurant menu won't give you nourishment. We've got to engage with what's offered if it's going to do us any good. But putting my heart in a place to receive truth certainly got me going in a completely different direction. This was a good place with good directions and solid friends I still have to this day.

Our decisions aren't just isolated choices. Our decisions point our lives in the directions we're about to head.

I didn't know how to chase down a decision at that point. But had I known, I would have seen how the bar scene would lead me to one place, and the church scene to the place I really needed to go.

Our decisions aren't just isolated choices. Our decisions point our lives in the directions we're about to head. Show me a decision and I'll show you a direction. We've got to get good at chasing down our decisions. See where they will take us. And make sure that's really where we want to go.

What's a decision you are in the midst of making? Chase it down. If you do this, where will it most likely lead? And then what? And then? Keep going until you walk it all the way out.

I know this may sound like a lot of work just to make a decision, but Proverbs 27:12 reminds us why it is so important to make sure we know the direction our lives are headed: "The prudent see danger and take refuge, but the simple keep going and pay the penalty."

This isn't meant to make you afraid to make the decision. It's to help you more clearly discern the package deal that comes with the decisions we make. And clarity should dispel the fear. I'd much prefer to know what I'm getting into than have it barreling toward me unaware.

Dear Lord, please give me insight to chase down the decision I'm facing. I want to understand where it might take me—and make a decision that will draw me closer to You. In Jesus' Name, Amen.

18

READ THIS BEFORE
MAKING THAT DECISION

"He who has compassion on them will guide them
and lead them beside springs of water."
—ISAIAH 49:10

*D*o you need to make a decision about something that seems so exciting, but you can't seem to shake the hesitation in your heart? Let's take a closer look at the idea of chasing down our decisions that we discussed yesterday.

We have a family friend named Wes who has been fascinated with pilots and planes since he was a little boy. For years, he dreamed of the life he's now living as a flight-school instructor.

It's thrilling. But recently it's all become a bit more complicated. The owner of the flight school decided to offer Wes the opportunity to buy him out. It's an amazing opportunity. But a scary one. One that created a bit of hesitation for Wes.

Our family has spent lots of time processing this decision with Wes. We've helped him with assessing the costs of this endeavor: the cost to him personally, the cost to his young wife, and the cost of everyday pressures people who own their own businesses feel.

As we were talking one day, I shared with him a picture I keep in my mind when making decisions.

Imagine this opportunity as an amazingly attractive but fast-moving river. There is so much that looks extremely appealing about this river, that you're going to be tempted to jump right in. But once in the river, you have diminished your ability to make decisions.

That river is moving so fast that it will take you where *it* is going. And if you haven't carefully determined in advance whether you want to go all the places the river flows, you'll be in trouble.

College students declaring their majors should trace the places that career will take them. If you think you want to major in chemistry but hate working in a lab or hospital, trace that river's path before jumping in.

Moms who are thinking about a new business opportunity should trace out all the expenses of getting started, including up-front costs, childcare, and inventory. If a mom's desire is to stay at home with the kids but this business will require her to be gone every night of the week, trace that river's path before jumping in.

Sometimes the greater act of faith is to let God lead us, talk to us, and instruct us beside the water.

Before jumping into the river, you have the ability to walk up and down the banks of the river with ease.

You have the ability to stick your toes in and consider what this water will be like.

You can talk to other wise people who know things about this river. And sit quietly listening for God's voice, reading His Word, and looking for confirmation on what to do next.

But once you jump in, the current has a way of demanding your full attention. It's not that you can't make adjustments once you're in the river; it's just a lot harder to go a different direction once you're in it.

Several verses describing God's leading, directing, and guiding *beside* the water have been great comfort to me:

- "He who has compassion on them will guide them and *lead them beside springs of water*" (Isaiah 49:10, emphasis mine).
- "The LORD is my shepherd; I shall not want. He makes me to lie down in green pastures; He *leads me beside the still waters*. He restores my soul; He leads me in the paths of righteousness for His name's sake" (Psalm 23:1–3 NKJV, emphasis mine).
- "With weeping they shall come, and with pleas for mercy I will lead them back, I will *make them walk by brooks of water*, in a straight path in which they shall not stumble, for I am a father to Israel" (Jeremiah 31:9, ESV, emphasis mine).

These verses are comforting to me because a lot is discussed in the Christian world about stepping out in faith—which I believe in wholeheartedly.

I believe God clearly instructs some to jump right in.

But that doesn't mean God calls everyone to jump right in. Sometimes the greater act of faith is to let God lead us, talk to us, and instruct us *beside* the water.

Dear Lord, I want to thoroughly think about this river before jumping in. Reveal anything I might not be seeing right now. In Jesus' Name, Amen.

19

Paralyzing Fear

Cast all your anxiety on him because he cares for you.
—1 Peter 5:7

The monkey bars were always the place on the playground I found most thrilling and most terrifying all at once. I watched the other kids laughing as they mindlessly romped up the ladder rungs to get to the first bar. Without a care, they let their bodies swing across from one bar to the next. It looked so effortless, and they seemed fearless and natural.

I wanted to join them. I wanted to play on the monkey bars more than any other piece of equipment on the whole playground.

But I was afraid.

I'd tried it once but it hadn't worked out so well. I'd held up the line. The longer the other monkey-bar climbers had to wait for me just hanging on the first bar, the more I could hear sighs. Cheeks full of air were being blown out behind me.

One boy got so tired of waiting he got his friend to hoist him up to the second bar and off he went. Others thought that was a great solution, so they followed suit. Suddenly not only was I afraid, I was embarrassed too.

All I had to do was release one hand from the first bar and thrust it forward to grab the next bar right in front of me. But I couldn't make my muscles move. No matter how hard I tried to will my hand to move, my thoughts paralyzed me. All I could think of were the bad things that could happen the minute my hand let go. So, there I stayed—for almost an entire recess.

A teacher finally saw what was happening and walked over to me. She placed her hands on my waist and helped me down. I know she thought she was helping me. But it felt like she was just agreeing with what I feared most: "You can't do this."

Falling would have been better. I could have gotten up from a physical fall. But being told that failure must be avoided at all costs kept me from ever getting back up on those monkey bars again. I would sit day after day staring from the swing across the playground. Watching other people do what I wanted to do.

Fear of all kinds can do this to us. We grab hold of it and don't let go. We want to overcome it, but we find ourselves hanging on that first bar, paralyzed from moving forward. Fear strangles the momentum that propelled us to grab the bar in the first place. There we stay, until someone hoists us down. And they lower us in more ways than one.

All those years ago on the playground, it would have been better if that teacher had just said, "Lysa, staying stuck in your fear is way worse than any other choice you could make right now. If you let go of that bar and happen to catch the next one, you'll move forward and prove to yourself that you can do this. Or, if you let go of that bar and fall, you'll see that the ground isn't so far away. It won't feel great to fall, but it won't be worse than all the stress and exhaustion you're experiencing just hanging there on the first bar."

Fear makes the gap between where I am and trusting God seem an impossible chasm.

Years later my youngest daughter Brooke was playing on the same kind of monkey bars with a friend and fell. When I took her to the doctor, he confirmed what the swelling in her arm had already told us. It was broken. But here's the amazing thing: Brooke's arm healed and she kept climbing the monkey bars.

I still won't attempt them.

I want to shift from trusting myself to trusting God, but how? Fear makes the gap between where I am and trusting God seem an impossible chasm.

But God doesn't want us to stay paralyzed in fear. And He has equipped us with comfort and reassurance. Over and over throughout the Bible, He tells us not to fear. The next time you find yourself clinging to your fear in a state of paralysis, remind yourself:

The Lord my God will be with me wherever I go (from Joshua 1:9).

God has redeemed me and summoned me by name. I am His (from Isaiah 43:1).

Nothing can ever separate me from the love of God (from Romans 8:38–39).

I can hand Him all my anxiety because He cares for me (from 1 Peter 5:7).

God gave us a spirit not of fear but of power and love and self-control (from 2 Timothy 1:7 ESV).

With the foundation of God's Word before us and beneath us, sweet sister, we can let go.

Dear heavenly Father, thank You for reminding me over and over not to fear. Lord, I hand over all my fears to You, and I will dwell on Your Word and Your strength. In Jesus' Name, Amen.

20

THE MOST NONFRANTIC
WOMAN I'VE EVER MET

A good name is more desirable than great riches;
to be esteemed is better than silver or gold.
—PROVERBS 22:1

*S*he was knocking at my front door trying to balance her paper coffee cup, her purse, her cell phone, and a stack of papers. She was also trying to fix something on her shoe. She hopped a step or two when I answered the door.

I smiled. Her imperfect posture delighted my mind that had been feeling a little off-kilter all morning. She smiled back and hopped one more time.

Finally, whatever was bugging her with her shoe seemed fixed. She stood up and smiled with an apologetic smile that made me adore her before we'd ever had our first conversation.

And with her first step over the threshold, it was as if the shoe issue never happened. She was noticeably focused on the project ahead of her.

She spent all day with my family and me. She was a reporter doing a story on our sons adopted from Africa. Even though she never alluded to another title she had, we knew.

She was the daughter of a former president of the United States. As in . . . she and her sister called the White House their home at one time. Her mom had been the first lady, which made her part of the first family.

The decisions we make, make the life we live.

But being the daughter of a president wasn't her role that day. She was a reporter. She was at our house to do a story. She stayed present in that role alone.

Her questions were honest and unassuming. Her demeanor kind. Her laugh delightfully loud. Her paperwork messy. But her focus was clear.

She was there to uncover a story.

So she stayed focused on the task at hand. She wasn't encumbered with a thousand other things pulling at her. She didn't try to multitask too much. She wasn't distracted by her cell phone. She wasn't running late or from one thing to the next.

She said no to everything else pulling at her. So she could say yes to the story. She gave it her Best Yes.

This woman who demonstrated a Best Yes that day left a lasting impression on my family for sure.

Later at dinner, the kids were asked to go around the table and say one word to describe the reporter.

"Nice."

"Humble."

"Classy."

"Elegant."

"Humble."

Then there may or may not have been a less than delightful exchange from an older sibling to the youngest child, "You can't say humble. I just said humble. You always want to copy what I have to say!"

I love family bonding.

But . . . I really did love the collective experience of meeting this nonfrantic woman. And the words my kids used to describe her.

The kids were then asked to explain what she did and how she carried herself that led us to use such great words to describe her.

If you want people to use such great words to describe you, think about the decisions you are making. How are they leading people to describe you? This question makes me think of Proverbs 22:1 which says, "A good name is more desirable than great riches; to be esteemed is better than silver or gold." I often encourage my kids with this truth when reminding them of the weight their decisions carry.

Yes, great descriptions are birthed from great decisions.

And better decisions help make better lives for those of us caught in craziness. Snagged. Worn out. Worn down. Ragged.

The decisions we make, make the life we live. So if we want to live better, we've got to decide better. Yes. No. The two most powerful words in the English language.

They can run us if we don't intentionally run them. Guard them. Guide them. Use yes and no to work for us. Can you imagine how great life would be if you didn't dread saying yes and felt completely empowered to say no?

Then and only then will our best selves emerge. And maybe you and I can start to be a little less frantic.

Dear Lord, I want to be described as a woman who says yes to You and to the assignments You have called me to. Help me to discern what those are today. In Jesus' Name, Amen.

21

THE TWO MOST POWERFUL WORDS

A voice from heaven said, "This is my Son,
whom I love; with him I am well pleased."
—MATTHEW 3:17

*N*ot too long ago, I stood at the sink trying to ease the stabbing feeling of stress. I had so much pulling at me.

I found myself rushing my loved ones in conversation. Rushing my kids out the door. Rushing to the next thing and then the next. Rushing to make dinner and then rushing my people through dinner.

I had set my life to the rhythm of rush.

Exhaustion gnawed deep places in my heart, demanding me to slow down. But how? I've made my decisions and now my decisions have made me. Me—this shell of a woman caught in the rush of endless demands.

Have you ever felt this same way? I suspect most of us have.

Like I said in yesterday's devotion, I'm starting to realize the two most powerful words are yes and no. How I use them determines how I set my schedule.

How I set my schedule determines how I live my life.

How I live my life determines how I spend my soul.

When I think about my decisions in light of spending my soul, it gives gravity to choosing more wisely. Each and every thing I say yes to sets the pace of my life.

After all, when a woman lives with the stress of an overwhelmed schedule, she'll ache with the sadness of an underwhelmed soul. An overwhelmed schedule leads to an underwhelmed soul—a soul with a full calendar but no time to really engage in life.

If you've found yourself caught in a stressful pace recently, I understand. I think so much of why my schedule gets overloaded is because I'm afraid of missing out or not measuring up.

One quick look at social media, and it feels like everyone else is able to live at a breakneck pace with a smile. Their kids are accomplishing more than my kids. Their business pursuits seem more important than mine do. Their home is cleaner. And they even have time to invite dinner guests over to eat food from their garden. Huh?

It's interesting to me the timing of God's words to Jesus in Matthew 3:17: "This is my Son, whom I love; with him I am well pleased."

At that point, Jesus hadn't yet performed miracles, led the masses, or gone to the cross. Yet, God was pleased with Jesus before all of those accomplishments.

His Father was establishing Jesus' identity before He started His activities. Jesus heard God, believed God, and remained unrushed. In Christ, God has given us a new identity (Romans 6:4). But, unlike Christ, we forget.

We fill our days and our lives with so much activity that the only way to keep up with it all is to rush. And I'm

When a woman lives with the stress of an overwhelmed schedule, she'll ache with the sadness of an underwhelmed soul.

discovering that the source of much of the stress in my life is this constant need to keep up. But what if I'm chasing the wrong desire?

Do I really want my life to look more like others'? Or to look more like God's best for me?

God's best for me means engaging with life and the people in it. God's best for me means noticing divine invitations and feeling the freedom to say yes—a Best Yes to the Lord's assignments.

If I really want an unrushed life, I must underwhelm my schedule so God has room to overwhelm my soul.

Today, we must stand moment by moment in the reality of our identity before we resume our activity. Grasp this truth and rub it in deep: "You are my daughter, whom I love; with whom I am well pleased."

Well pleased because of who you are, not because of what you do. Well pleased because of an unfathomable, unconditional love that's not earned, but simply given.

Dear Lord, unrush me as I set my schedule today. I want to step out of the rush so I can embrace Your best for me. In Jesus' Name, Amen.

22

ANALYSIS PARALYSIS

The Spirit helps us in our weakness. We do not know what
we ought to pray for, but the Spirit himself intercedes for us
through wordless groans. And he who searches our hearts
knows the mind of the Spirit, because the Spirit intercedes
for God's people in accordance with the will of God. And we
know that in all things God works for the good of those who
love him, who have been called according to his purpose.
—ROMANS 8:26–28

Maybe you have been there. A decision needs to be made. You ponder and pray. You research and get other people's opinions. You analyze the hows and what-ifs. You desperately want to know which is the one right decision to make. The perfect move. The will of God.

Not being able to make a decision is a feverish symptom but not the real sickness. Fear of failure is the real cause of our analysis paralysis.

We should fear stepping out of God's will. But if you desire to please God with the decision you make and afterward it proves to be a mistake, it's an error not an end.

It took me quite awhile to get this. I remember being a young girl wondering how in the world I'd make all the right choices in life. What if I picked the wrong college? And then picked the wrong town to move to after college? And then picked the wrong job that put me in the wrong circle of friends? And then and then and . . . a thousand more mistakes that all spun off picking the wrong college. I would analyze every option until I didn't want to make any decision for fear of making the wrong one.

> God's promises are not dependent on my ability to always choose well, but rather on His ability to use well.

I have a friend who had this same analysis paralysis until a wise mentor said something that gave her freedom. He said so many people stress over knowing God's will and what the right choice is. But sometimes God gives us two or more choices that would all please Him and be in His will. We get to choose.

My friend said understanding that has given her more confidence to make decisions, In fact, it's strengthened her relationship with God as she exercises stepping out in faith, trusting God to give her the discernment she needs to choose wisely.

The fear of making a wrong decision shouldn't strip the faith right out of our faith. The only way our faith will ever strengthen is for us to use it. We need to apply thought and prayer to our decisions and then trust God for the outcome. We need to set our sights on growing in faith, not shrinking back for fear of failure.

If I'm trusting myself, I will stare at all the possible ways I could fail. If I'm trusting God, I will stare at all the possible ways He'll use this whether I fail or succeed. When I stare at failure, I'll fear it. I'll convince myself it's the worst thing that could happen. And I'll stay stuck. But when I stare at all the possible ways God can use this whether I succeed or fail, I'll face my decision. I'll convince myself that it's better to step out and find out than to stay stuck.

Here's the bottom line. Good decisions will often have elements of not so good. And not-so-good decisions have elements of good. Either way, if I'm hoping to be able to know the perfect choice and then move forward with absolute certainty, I'll probably not move forward.

Here's where the certainty is: My imperfections will never override God's promises. God's promises are not dependent on my ability to always choose well, but rather on His ability to use well.

God will use the good and not-so-good parts of the decisions we make. A very popular verse reminds us of this. Romans 8:28 says, "And we know that in all things God works for the good of those who love him, who have been called according to his purpose."

Don't miss this crucial part: "for the good of those who love him." We must have at the core of our hearts a love for God and a surrender to God if we want to be guided by God.

Also don't miss the context from which this verse is pulled. Verse 28 starts with the word *and*, which tells me that it's tied to the verses that precede it. Verses 26–27 remind us that when we are feeling uncertain or weak, the Holy Spirit will lift up prayers for us in accordance to God's will. Let's read the whole paragraph as it goes together.

"The Spirit helps us in our weakness. We do not know what we ought to pray for, but the Spirit himself intercedes for us through wordless groans. And he who searches our hearts knows the mind of the Spirit, because the Spirit intercedes for God's people in accordance with the will of God. And we know that in all things God works for the good of those who love him, who have been called according to his purpose" (vv. 26–28).

If your heart and your mind are aligned in the direction of God, you don't have to agonize to the point of paralysis over the decisions before you. We will steer where we stare. So stare mightily at God and His plan. And if you don't know His plan, stare mightily at living out His Word in your life, and His plan will unfold day by day. Decision by decision.

God, thank You for being sovereign over my life. Thank You for Your Word to guide me. I ask the Holy Spirit to intercede on my behalf, and I commit my decisions to You. Thank You, Father. In Jesus' Name, Amen

23

FIVE QUESTIONS TO
ASK WHEN MAKING A DECISION

"Which of you, intending to build a tower, does not sit
down first and count the cost, whether he has enough to
finish it—lest, after he has laid the foundation, and is not
able to finish, all who see it begin to mock him, saying,
'This man began to build and was not able to finish'?"
—LUKE 14:28–30 NKJV

I wasn't in the mood to take on the stress of making another decision. I was just so tired. So spent. Not in the mood to deal with one
more thing.

A family friend in her early twenties was looking to move out of
her apartment and into a less expensive living situation. We adore this
young lady. She's spent a lot of time with our family. She's lovely and
no trouble at all.

However, when she asked to move in with us, I felt a deep sense of
caution. I'd been helping one of my kids through a difficult situation
that required a lot of my time and emotional energy.

But maybe I could do this, too, I thought. My heart was certainly
saying yes. But my heart and my reality don't always line up.

So, I knew I needed to take myself through a process of evaluating
this decision. And my evaluation would have to include my capacity.

It's good to use wisdom, knowledge, and an understanding of
your resource capacity to assess your decisions.

In fact, Luke 14:28–30 encourages it: "Which of you, intending to build a tower, does not sit down first and count the cost, whether he has enough to finish it—lest, after he has laid the foundation, and is not able to finish, all who see it begin to mock him, saying, 'This man began to build and was not able to finish'?"

I ran this situation through the filter of five questions:

1. Do I have the resources to handle this request along with my current responsibilities?
2. Could this fit physically?
3. Could this fit financially?
4. Could this fit spiritually?
5. Could this fit emotionally?

I dug through my purse to retrieve the only paper I could find—a random receipt. I scrawled out a list of things to consider when making this decision.

Did saying yes to this make sense in each of these areas?

- *Physically?* We had a spare bedroom.
- *Financially?* Her small rent payment would cover any additional expenses.
- *Spiritually?* We are Christians, and we want to love other people. This seemed to fall right in line with our core values.

But there was one more aspect to be considered. Could I handle this emotionally? Did I really have the white space to do this and keep an attitude of love?

This is where I felt the most caution. Remember how I was feeling at the time? So tired. So spent.

I've learned to pay attention to my emotional capacity and be honest with myself when I'm stretched too thin. When I allow myself to get overloaded emotionally, the worst version of me emerges. And that's not good for anyone.

As I continued to count the cost and assess my available resources, I felt I should say no. But I also felt I was expected to say yes. Do I go with what I'm expected to do? Or what I feel I should do?

It's good to use wisdom, knowledge, and an understanding of your resource capacity to assess your decisions.

Whenever there is a conflict between what we feel we're expected to do and what we feel we should do, it's time to step back from the decision and seek clarity from the only source free from entanglements: God.

Praying for wisdom and considering these five questions gave me a peace that God would be her provider. Therefore, my saying yes when I knew I should say no would prevent her from experiencing His best provision.

Amazingly, when I called her to explain why this wouldn't work, she was giddy with excitement over an apartment she'd found that was right in line with her budget.

God provided. He provided my friend with a great living situation. He provided me with another assurance that not every opportunity was meant to be my assignment.

Dear Lord, thank You for providing wisdom whenever we ask for it. Please guide me in the decisions I need to make today. In Jesus' Name, Amen.

24

GOD, I'M WORN OUT

When I am overwhelmed,
you alone know the way I should turn.
—PSALM 142:3 NLT

*H*ave you ever had one of those late-night come-to-Jesus moments where the weight of regret lays heavy across your chest?

For me, it usually happens because in the hectic pace of the day, I blew up at a loved one, I brushed past a moment of connection with someone God put in my path, or I rushed through all the moments without stopping to enjoy them.

I've discovered a great source of stress, distraction, and exhaustion in my life. I say yes to too many things. I take on too many good things, which causes me to miss my best things. It's so hard to say no and let go of opportunities that come my way. But if I don't learn the gift of release, I'll wrestle with a lack of peace.

I saw this visibly a few years ago when I traveled to visit a friend. As soon as she picked me up from the airport and we started driving, I saw the fallout from a massive twenty-inch snow in the middle of fall. But it wasn't the amount of snow still on the ground that grabbed my attention.

It was the broken trees. The branches were piled everywhere, all still clinging to the leaves that hadn't dropped yet. And because the leaves hadn't dropped, the trees broke.

That's what happens when a snow comes early. The trees weren't designed to face snow before releasing their leaves. They weren't made to carry more than they should. And neither are we.

I know the weight of carrying more than I should. And usually it's because I've refused to release something before taking on something else.

We see how refusing to release gets people in trouble all throughout Scripture.

Eve refused to release the forbidden fruit. And because she became hyperfocused on that one thing, she missed out on the best things in paradise.

Refusing to release often means refusing to have peace.

Esau refused to release his urgent need for some stew. And because he became hyperfocused on eating that soup, he missed out on his birthright.

Moses refused to release his fear that just speaking to the rock as God commanded wouldn't actually bring forth water. And because he struck the rock twice, he missed out on entering the promised land.

Each of these people paid a high price for their refusals to release—to let go of their ways so they could walk in the amazing way of God.

It wasn't God's desire for any of these people to suffer the consequences they did. Each of us has a free will, which means we have the freedom to make choices.

God tells us the right way to go, but we have to make the choice to do so. Choices and consequences come in package deals. When we make a choice, we ignite the consequences that can come along with it.

It was true for Eve, Esau, and Moses. And it's true for you and me. Refusing to release often means refusing to have peace. I trade my peace for a weight of regret.

Release is a gift to a woman weighed down, grasping her leaves in the midst of a snowstorm, so desperate for help. She can feel the twinges and hear the creaking sounds of a splitting break about to happen.

She knows she can't take much more. She remembers Psalm 142:3, "When I am overwhelmed, you alone know the way I should turn." Tears well up in her upturned, pleading eyes. *God, help me. It's all too much. I'm tired and frustrated and so very worn out.*

The wind whips past her, trailing a whispered, "R-e-l-e-a-s-e." She must listen or she will break. Her tree needs to be stripped and prepared for winter. But she can't embrace winter until she lets go of fall. Like a tree, a woman can't carry the weight of two seasons simultaneously. In the violent struggle of trying, she'll miss every bit of joy each season promises to bring.

Release brings with it the gift of peace. There are some opportunities I need to decline today. There are some things I need to say no to in this current season. There are good things I need to let go of so I can make room for the best things. Then and only then can my beautiful, bare winter branch receive its snow. When we release in peace, we signal we're now ready to receive what's meant for this season, right now.

So let's release. With release comes more peace. I see that now. I believe that now. And soon, I pray, you will too.

Dear Lord, only You can help me with this release.
My heart seeks to obey You. In Jesus' Name, Amen.

25

In the Flow

His divine power has given us everything we need
for a godly life through our knowledge of him
who called us by his own glory and goodness.
—2 Peter 1:3

When my kids were growing up, my family and I spent a week each summer at a camp tucked in the Adirondack Mountains. It was an amazing get-away. Great chapel preaching every morning, no TV, beautiful lake, campfires, fishing, putt-putt golf, shuffleboard, and more game playing than you can imagine.

Nature erupts with untarnished beauty and begs to be explored. So, one year, when my exercise-loving friends we vacation with suggested we join them for a moderate family hike, we agreed.

Well, their definition of the word *moderate* and mine didn't come from the same dictionary. Actually, not from the same planet if I'm being completely honest. Honey, honey, honey . . . this was no *moderate* hike.

I pictured a path with a gentle, winding, upward slope.

What we actually hiked was a full-on upward scaling of rocks and roots.

Not kidding.

In an altitude where the air seemed so thin the inside of my lungs felt like they were sticking together and refusing my chest full breaths. Lovely.

Up, up, up we went. And when another group passed us on their way down and cheerfully quipped, "You're almost halfway there," I wanted to quit. *Halfway?* How could we only be halfway!?!

I pushed. I pulled. I strained. I huffed and puffed. And I might have even spent a few minutes pouting.

But eventually, we reached the top. I bent over holding my sides wondering how a girl who runs almost every day of her life could be so stinkin' out of shape! Going up against the pull of gravity was hard. Really, really hard.

But coming down was a completely different experience. We navigated the same rocks and roots without feeling nearly as stressed. I enjoyed the journey. I noticed more of the beautiful surroundings and had enough breath to talk to those with me all the way down.

And about halfway down the trail, it occurred to me how similar this hike was to the Christian walk.

Starting at the top, working with the pull of gravity was so much easier than starting at the bottom and working against it.

Seeking to obey God in the midst of whatever circumstance I'm facing will position me to work in the flow of God's power.

Though we navigated the exact same path both directions, going in the flow of gravity made the journey so much better.

Just like when I face an issue in life, operating *in the flow* of God's power is so much better than working *against* the flow of God's power.

In other words, seeking to obey God in the midst of whatever circumstance I'm facing will position me to work in the flow of God's power. I'll still have to navigate the realities of my situation, but I won't be doing it with my strength.

My job is to be obedient to God. Apply His Word. Walk according to His ways—not the world's suggestions. Participate in His divine nature rather than wallow in my own bad attitude and insecurities.

Then I won't have to huff and puff and pout while trying to figure everything out. I stay in the flow. God, in His way and timing, works it all out.

So, the question of the day . . . will we work in or out of the flow today? Go with the flow of God's power. 2 Peter 1:3 tells us, "His divine power has given us everything we need for a godly life through our knowledge of him who called us by his own glory and goodness." Wow. When I let that sink in, I'm so inspired to handle everything I face today the way God instructs. Everything!

And if you're thinking of asking me on a hike, I require pictures of the path first. Okay?

Dear Lord, help me to operate in the flow of Your power today and not against it. Your divine power has given me everything I need for a godly life. I believe this truth today. In Jesus' Name, Amen.

26

PRACTICING WISDOM

My son, if you accept my words
  and store up my commands within you,
turning your ear to wisdom
  and applying your heart to understanding . . .
  and search for it as for hidden treasure,
then you will understand the fear of the LORD
  and find the knowledge of God.

—PROVERBS 2:1–2, 4–5

My daughter Ashley was a pole-vaulter in high school. She learned how to sprint down the track in spiked shoes, plant the very long pole she's carrying into a small pit, bend the pole down enough to create a force to lift her body off the ground, twist so her head is down and her feet are now pointed toward the sky, arch over a bar at least eight feet off the mat, and throw the pole away from her at the last minute while she crashes down onto the mat, hopefully back-first and not face-first.

Whew.

Did I mention she had to do all that without jostling or hitting the bar she was careening over, lest the bar fall and her jump not count? It's no joke.

Her first and second years of pole vaulting were hard. She held last place on the team most of the time.

But as she got into her third year, some things finally clicked. She moved up to being consistently ranked second on her team. And then something amazing happened.

At a meet one day, she was taking her turn to vault over nine feet six inches. I could tell she was nervous. Really nervous.

She missed the first attempt and then the second.

As she limped to the starting place for another try, I could feel the tension, the nerves, the pressure. When she finally broke into the sprint down the track, nothing looked any different from any other time she'd run. When she planted her pole, nothing looked any different from any other time she'd planted her pole. But when she cleared ten feet with ease, the expression on her face was so very different from any expression I'd ever seen.

She popped off the mat and erupted in a jubilant scream I'll never forget. She ran from behind the mat straight into the arms of a mama who may or may not have been making a slight spectacle of herself. Screams of joy. Tears of amazement.

It was mind-blowing. This girl, who for years struggled in this sport, took first in the meet and was now the new school-record holder.

As her mama I'm proud of her accomplishment. But you know what makes me most proud? The fact she just kept showing up at practice and giving it her all.

Run after run. Attempt after attempt. Day after day. Sometimes succeeding, sometimes failing, sometimes feeling great, sometimes in pain, most times in last place—but no matter what, she was committed

Wisdom needs to be practiced day after day if we are going to know how to apply it to decisions when they come.

to showing up to practice. And the same can be true for us if we want to know how to make godly decisions.

If we want to know what to do when it matters most, we've got to be committed to showing up to practice. Wisdom needs to be practiced day after day if we are going to know how to apply it to decisions when they come.

Likewise, we've got to train our wisdom muscles to be strong and capable so when we need them most, we'll know how to use wisdom.

Proverbs 2:1–11 gives us clear instruction on the way to have wisdom, use wisdom, and be protected by wisdom.

- Accept God's words. (God's Word is a gift. But it won't do us any good if we don't accept the gift, open the gift, and use the gift.)
- Store up His commands within us. (We must get into God's Word and let God's Word get into us. The more verses we memorize, the more our thinking will align with His truth.)
- Turn our ears to wisdom. (Listen to wise teaching, wise advice, and keep the company of wise people.)
- Call out for insight. (Ask others to help us see the consequences we'd be igniting with each choice.)
- Cry aloud for understanding. (Ask the Lord to show us how our choices will affect others.)
- Look for wisdom as passionately as we would hunt for a hidden treasure. (See the value of wisdom as higher than that of any worldly way we are offered. Stay focused on looking for wisdom despite the many distractions the world puts in front of us that would cause us to make decisions without taking the time to apply sought-after wisdom.)

After all these qualifiers, the Scriptures say, "Then you will understand the fear of the LORD and find the knowledge of God. For the LORD gives wisdom; from his mouth come knowledge and understanding" (vv. 5–6).

Sweet friend, I'm cheering you on from here. You've got this.

Just show up to practice. Practice godly wisdom with all you've got in you. And let your mind do what it knows to do from all that practice.

God, thank You for Your wisdom. Help me to show up for practice each and every day with a willing heart and an eager spirit. I love You. In Jesus' Name, Amen.

Part 2

Embracing the Fullness Found Only in Him

27

What Holds the Key to Your Heart?

When Jesus heard this, he said to him, "You still lack one
thing. Sell everything you have and give to the poor, and
you will have treasure in heaven. Then come, follow me."

—LUKE 18:22

I long to be a woman who follows hard after Jesus. And I'm not talking about a plastic-Christian life, full of religious checklists and
pretense. No, that would be hypocritical at best and deadening at
worst.

I want the kind of soul-satisfying closeness that can only come
from daily keeping pace with Him. A rich and deep level of intimacy
that frantic attempts at rule-following will never produce.

Rules and regulations were an everyday reality for God's people in
the Old Testament. Lists of dos and don'ts to help sinful people main-
tain fellowship with a holy God. First the Ten Commandments. Then
law after law about sacrifices and ceremonies, food and cleanliness.

But in the New Testament, Jesus shows up on the scene and turns
everything upside down with His message of grace. A message that
declares, "Following rules won't get you into heaven. Being good won't
earn you bonus points. Lay down your checklists . . . your agendas . . .
everything . . . and follow Me. Believe in Me. Receive Me."

It was a complete shift in thinking. One that left people perplexed,
like the rich ruler in Luke 18.

We first meet the rich ruler when he approaches Jesus with a question: "Good teacher, what must I do to inherit eternal life?" (Luke 18:18).

Jesus, already knowing his checklist-mindset, begins naming several of the Ten Commandments. It's a list the rich ruler feels he has kept well. But Jesus has more to say: "You still lack one thing. Sell everything you have and give to the poor, and you will have treasure in heaven. Then come, follow me" (Luke 18:22).

Let's be found captured by Jesus' love, enthralled with His teachings, and living proof of His truth.

It would be so easy to gloss over this moment and think Jesus is simply talking about money. We could be tempted to label this a story for "those" people—the ones we think have more money than they know what to do with. But the words in this conversation are for every single one of us. Because the core issue Jesus is getting at is this: *What holds the key to your heart?*

Oh, how I want my answer to be "Jesus." I want to want Him most. To live completely captured by His love. Enthralled with His teachings. Living proof of His truth.

There have been others who have gone before me who desired this as well. Imperfect heroes of faith we read about in the Bible who, despite their shortcomings, pleased God. And it wasn't perfect actions that carved a path to God's heart. It was something else. Something less defined that can't be outlined and dissected. Something that was sometimes messy and offensive. But something that was so precious at the same time it caused God to pause.

Abandon.

It's a word used to describe a little girl leaping from the bed's edge, completely confident her daddy will catch her. It's the same thing that fueled David's courageous run toward Goliath with nothing but a sling and five smooth stones. It's what fueled Joshua. And Moses. And Noah. And Paul.

And it's the one thing Jesus is asking of the rich ruler. Not for a life lived perfectly, but a heart of perfect surrender. So this is my prayer:

Everything I have. Everything I own. Everything I hope for. Everything I fear. Everything I love. Everything I dream. It's all Yours, Jesus. I trust You in complete and utter abandon.

Sadly, it's also the one thing this man felt he could not offer. He stood on the edge of everything uncertain with the arms of all certainty waiting to catch him. And he just couldn't jump; he lived his life entangled in lesser things.

He was not captured by, enthralled with, or living proof of the reality of Jesus. And so he walked away from the only One who could ever truly satisfy his soul.

Oh, friends. Let's not allow this to be the tragedy of our lives. Let's be found captured by Jesus' love, enthralled with His teachings, and living proof of His truth. Let's be found living with abandon.

Because the life that follows Jesus with abandon is the life that gets to experience His presence, His provision, His promises, His soul-satisfying abundance.

Father God, please forgive me for all of the times I have settled for lesser things. I want to want You most. Today, I am handing You the key to my heart. The key to everything in my life. I love You. I need You. And I want to follow hard after You. In Jesus' Name, Amen.

28

THE MOST SEARCHED-FOR ANSWER

Salvation is found in no one else, for there is no other name
under heaven given to mankind by which we must be saved.
—ACTS 4:12

*G*rowing up, I had a plan for how I could make my life good.

Get a good education. A good job. A good family. A good house. A good flower bed out front. And a good minivan parked in the driveway.

Then life would be . . . good.

Eventually, I had all that good stuff. I was thankful for it all. I loved my family to pieces. The minivan wasn't all I thought it would be, but I felt like an official mom driving it. So even that wound up being good.

But something inside me still felt hollow. A little off. A little lacking.

So, I reasoned I needed something else to do. A place where I could use my gifts and talents. And while these things were fun and satisfying on one level, they too fell short when it came to that deep place ringing with the echoes of empty.

Empty is a heavy load to bear. The mystery of wanting to be filled but not knowing how or what could fill the deep longing of our soul is a gnawing ache. A search that can seem both futile and shattering at times.

When you try and try, always feeling like the answer is just around the corner, and then it isn't, it can split your heart wide open and leak dry all your reserves.

It can make you feel unsatisfied and frustrated with everything. Even those you love. Maybe especially those you love.

So you fake a smile and keep putting one foot in front of the other. But eventually you stop peeking around the next corner hoping the answer is there. History tells you it isn't. And wrapped in that perception is the noose that strangles out all hope.

Sadly, this is where many women live.

I know this place because I lived there. I struggled there.

It quite honestly stinks.

So, I'm not going to pretend you'll suddenly feel super terrific after reading this.

But what I can promise is a string of words that explains a lot. An answer that is sure and solid and true and full of the breathless wonder of a hope rediscovered.

Salvation can't be found in anyone or anything else. There is no other. Only Jesus.

"Salvation is found in no one else, for there is no other name under heaven given to mankind by which we must be saved" (Acts 4:12).

No good plan is the answer.

No education or job or house can save you.

Salvation can't be found in anyone or anything else.

There is no other.

Only Jesus.

And I'm not just talking about saying we're Christians. Following the rules and following Jesus are two totally different things.

Going through the motions of religion won't ever satisfy. It's only when we bend down low, open our hearts in complete surrender, and say, "Jesus, it's You. Only You. There is no other. There is no other possession or person or position that can ever fill the deep soul-place shaped only for You."

This is my prayer. Though I've been saved for a long time, I want to recapture the essence of this "no other" reality.

And really live like this is true.

Because it is. True.

Jesus, only You can save and fill and give what my soul desires. Please remind me to draw close to You and rely on the promise that You will draw close to me when I do. In Jesus' Name, Amen.

29

If Only I Had . . .

The law of the LORD is perfect,
   reviving the soul;
the testimony of the LORD is sure,
   making wise the simple;
the precepts of the LORD are right,
   rejoicing the heart;
the commandment of the LORD is pure,
   enlightening the eyes.

—PSALM 19:7–8 ESV

There's a simple, yet incredibly dangerous little script many of us play in our minds. It might even be one of the biggest things that holds us back from feeling fulfilled in our relationship with God. It's a script tangled in a lie that typically goes something like this: *I could really be happy and fulfilled if only I had . . .*

. . . a skinnier body.

. . . more money.

. . . a better personality.

. . . a baby.

I don't know what your "If only I had" statements are, but I do know this: none of them will bring fulfillment. They might bring temporary moments of happiness, but not true fulfillment. Apart from a thriving relationship with God, even if we got everything on our list, there would still be a hollow gap in our soul.

So instead of saying, "If only I had" and filling in the blank with some person, possession, or position, we must make the choice to replace that statement with God's truth. Psalm 19:7–8 confirms just how powerful and beneficial the truth of God's Word is: "The law of the LORD is perfect, reviving the soul; the testimony of the LORD is sure, making wise the simple; the precepts of the LORD are right, rejoicing the heart; the commandment of the LORD is pure, enlightening the eyes."

Our soul was tailor-made to be filled with God and His truth.

Here are some examples that have helped me battle the temptation to let people, possessions, or positions take God's place in my life.

People.

I no longer say, "If only I had a daddy who loved me." Instead, I say, "Psalm 68:5 promises God is a father to the fatherless."

Maybe your gap isn't left by an absent father but by a friend who hurt you. Or the children you've longed to have, and you still don't. Whatever that gap is, God is the perfect fit for your emptiness.

Pray this paraphrase of Luke 1:78–79: "Because of the tender mercy of my God by which the rising sun will come to me from heaven—to shine on my darkness and in what feels like the shadow of death to me—I will find peace."

Possessions.

I no longer say, "If only I had more possessions." Instead, I recite Matthew 6:19–21: "Do not store up for yourselves treasures on earth, where moth and rust destroy, and where thieves break in and steal. But store up for yourselves treasures in heaven, where neither moth nor rust destroys, and where thieves do not break in and steal. For where your treasure is, there your heart will be also" (NASB).

Any possession I ever long for, no matter how good it may seem, will only be good for a limited time. In light of eternity, every possession is in the process of breaking down, becoming devalued, and will eventually be taken from us. If I set my heart solely on acquiring more things, I'll feel more vulnerable with the possibility of loss.

Possessions are meant to be appreciated and used to bless others. They were never meant to be identity markers. It's not wrong to enjoy the possessions we have as long as we don't depend on them for our heart's security.

Position.

I no longer say, "If only I had a better position." Instead, I say the words of Psalm 119:105, "Your word is a lamp to my feet and a light for my path" (NASB). I don't need a better position to get where I should go. I don't have to figure out my path and strive to get ahead. I need God's Word to guide me. As I follow Him and honor Him step-by-step, I can be assured that I'm right where He wants me, to be doing what He wants me to do.

Whatever "If only I had" statement you're struggling with, you can replace it with solid truths from Scripture that will never leave you empty.

When God's Word gets inside of us, it becomes the new way we process life. It rearranges our thoughts, our motives, our needs, and our desires. Our soul was tailor-made to be filled with God and His truth; therefore, it seeps into every part of us and fills us completely.

Dear Lord, I acknowledge only You can fill those empty places in my heart. Help me stop the "If only I had" cycle and instead be set free with Your truth. In Jesus' Name, Amen.

30

The Seduction of Satisfaction

*My God will meet all your needs according
to his glorious riches in Christ Jesus.*
—Philippians 4:19

Have you ever been tempted to make seemingly small compromises in the short term that had the potential to take you away from God's best in the long term?

I know this struggle all too well. But I also know that those *small* compromises build upon one another until they become a *big* pile of regret.

Temptation of any kind is Satan's invitation to get our needs met outside the will of God.

One of the subtle ways he does this is to plant the hesitant thought in our mind that God will not meet our needs—that God is not enough. Satan wants us to feel alone and abandoned, so that we turn to his offerings instead. It's the seduction of satisfaction.

Often the script that plays in our head is like the one I mentioned in yesterday's devotion, *I need _____ so I can be satisfied.*

It's what sends the wife on a budget off on a spending spree. She feels the thrill of the sale in the moment. But as she's hiding the bags from her husband, shame creeps in.

It's what pulls at the businesswoman to work harder and longer and refuse to build boundaries in her schedule. Always chasing that next accomplishment or that next compliment, but it's never enough.

It's what sent me on many eating sprees. The kids were loud, the house was messy, the demands felt beyond my control. So with great justification I'd indulge, only to have a bloated stomach and a deflated heart.

This subtle message sold to us by Satan can be exposed when we understand the difference between a *need* and a *want*.

> *Satan's temptation drains life. God's provision sustains life.*

All of the examples above were wants—not needs. But oh, how Satan wants to make them one and the same.

When the difference between these two words starts getting skewed, we start compromising. We start justifying. And it sets us up to start getting our needs met outside the will of God. The abyss of discontentment invites us in and threatens to darken and distort everything in our world.

Listen: Satan is a liar. The more we fill ourselves with his distorted desires, the emptier we'll feel. That's true with each of the desires mentioned above. The more we overspend, overwork, or overeat—the emptier we feel. Remember, Satan wants to separate you from God's best plans. He wants to separate you from God's proper provision. He wants to separate you from God's peace.

Satan's temptation drains life. *God's provision sustains life.*

Satan's temptation in the short term will reap heartache in the long term. *God's provision in the short term will reap blessings in the long term.*

Satan's temptation gratifies the flesh. *God's provision satisfies the soul.*

Oh, sweet sister, we must consider these realities when making choices today. We're all just a few poor choices away from doing things we never thought we would. Especially when our hearts are in a vulnerable place of longing for something that God hasn't yet provided.

And the time to prevent destruction from temptation is before it ever starts.

We are either holding fast to God's promise or being lured by a compromise. And isn't it interesting that the word *promise* is right there in the midst of that word *com(promise)*?

God promises, "I will meet all your needs according to the riches of My Glory in Christ Jesus" (Philippians 4:19, paraphrased). He is everything we need and so perfectly capable of filling in the gaps of our wants as well. We must let truth seep deep into the longings of our soul. Otherwise lies are prone to creep into this place of our desire.

Yes. We must trust God. Embrace truth. Live His promise.

Dear Lord, help me focus only on Your provision in my life today. I don't want to be separated from You, Your best plans for me, or Your peace. Help me notice when the Enemy is trying to entice me with false desires, because they only lead to emptiness. In Jesus' Name, Amen.

31

The Pathway to Humility

He humbled you, causing you to hunger and then feeding
you with manna, which neither you nor your ancestors had
known, to teach you that man does not live on bread alone
but on every word that comes from the mouth of the Lord.

—Deuteronomy 8:3

A friend of mine who is a young leader at a growing organization recently told me about some discouragement he'd been wrestling through. Basically, he'd been working so hard, seen great success, but was given no recognition or encouragement by his leaders. And hardest of all, due to some transitions in the company, he'd been demoted to a lower position.

I asked him a seemingly strange question on the heels of his admission: "Do you know what the opposite of pride is?"

He tilted his head and asked his own question, "Do you think I'm struggling with pride?"

I wasn't trying to imply my young friend was prideful. I was setting the stage to help him see his circumstances through a different lens.

So I simply stated, "I believe the opposite of pride is trust in God. Pride begs us to believe it all depends on us. Trusting God requires us to place our dependence on Him. And the pathway that leads us away from pride and into a place of truly trusting God is paved with

> *Humility will always cost us something but will be worth the price we pay.*

humility. Humility is never bought at a cheap price. It will always cost us something but will be worth the price we pay.

"Might God be using these humbling circumstances to get you to a place of deep and unshakable trust in Him? If God sees big things ahead for you, and I believe He does, then He must remove all hints of pride. Even if pride is but a tiny thorn in your heart now, when you are given a bigger position with more recognition, that pride will grow from a thorn to a dagger with the potential to kill your calling."

In the Old Testament, we see God revealing this same kind of pride-stripping process by feeding the children of Israel manna in the desert for the purpose of humbling them. It was crucial that God prepare them to trust Him as they stepped from the desert into their destined promised land.

Deuteronomy 8:2 says, "Remember how the LORD your God led you all the way in the wilderness these forty years, to humble and test you in order to know what was in your heart, whether or not you would keep his commands."

And then our key verse Deuteronomy 8:3 goes on to reveal, "He humbled you, causing you to hunger and then feeding you with manna, which neither you nor your ancestors had known, to teach you that man does not live on bread alone but on every word that comes from the mouth of the LORD."

So why exactly was having to eat manna so humbling? And what can we glean from Deuteronomy 8:3 for our own lives today?

Here are three things I think we can take away from today's key verse:

1. God is our provider. The children of Israel were used to looking down at the ground in Egypt and working the land to provide for themselves. They trusted their own hard work for their provision. Now, they would need to look up and trust God for His provision.

2. God's provision is what we need but not always what we want. This manna God provided was not like the normal food the Israelites were used to providing for themselves. But God knew it was the perfect nourishment for those in the desert. He knows our needs better than we do. God is more concerned about our ultimate good than our temporary pleasure.

3. God's provision protects our hearts. Our desires have the potential of corrupting our hearts. Man-made bread is not what gives the fullness of life God desires for us. Man-made success, riches, and popularity are the same way. They will not fulfill us like we think they will. Only the Word of God can seep into the hungry places of our souls and make the dead and discouraged places within come fully alive and deeply satisfied. We must want Him most of all. And then He will see our hearts are prepared and trustworthy to handle other things.

At the end of our discussion, my young friend thanked me for helping him see that in each hard step of his journey as a leader, he's either walking the pathway of pride, by trusting himself, *or* the pathway of humility, which is trusting God. And the same is true for each of us.

May we all choose to trust Him and let that be the lens through which we process our circumstances. May we see how God isn't trying to break our hearts but rather make us ready for what He sees just ahead.

Lord, thank You for caring so deeply for me. Search my heart for any shred of pride. And help me live a life of humble and complete surrender to You. In Jesus' Name, Amen.

32

WHAT ARE YOU MISSING?

The LORD looks down from heaven on all mankind to see
if there are any who understand, any who seek God.
—PSALM 14:2

A few summers ago, my son Mark was working at a family camp. While the mountains were breathtaking, the friends were plentiful, and the food was every teenager's dream, he missed home. Not horribly—but just enough to tug on the vulnerable places of his heart.

I knew he needed some sweet comfort from home. So, I packaged up some things he needed and a few items I knew would make him happy and sent my gift of love.

After a few days, I kept wondering when I'd get a text from him with smiles and "Thank you!" and "Wow! You're the best mom ever!" messages. *A girl can dream, right?*

But no text message came.

Each day that went by, I grew more and more frustrated by his lack of acknowledgment of my gift. I started to wonder if he'd even received it.

I finally got ahold of Mark and asked him about the package, and he answered, "Oh yeah, I did get a box, but I haven't opened it yet."

Huh?

Who receives a gift of love packaged up and sent to them and doesn't even take the time to open it?

In that moment, I felt the Holy Spirit prick my soul, "Lysa, sometimes you do this very same thing. Oh, if you only knew the number of experiences God Himself has packaged up and sent your way that you didn't take time to open . . .

"Or the number of times God has planted a bunch of wildflowers at the end of your driveway just to make you smile, but in the rush of where you were headed, you didn't notice . . .

Seeking requires me to sacrifice the things I feel compelled to chase so I can be available to notice God's clear direction.

"Or the number of times God has treasures in His Word waiting for you to uncover that would perfectly prepare you for something you'd be facing that day, if only you'd lingered with Him a little longer."

Today's key verse, Psalm 14:2, reminds us, "The LORD looks down from heaven on all mankind to see if there are any who understand, any who seek God."

I wish this verse were worded differently. I wish this verse read: "The LORD looks down from heaven to see *many* who understand, *many* who seek God." But that's not the reality of the verse. And sadly, sometimes in the rush of all I feel I must do, it's not the reality of my life.

I want it to be. But my soul is so prone to distractions.

Seeking—really seeking—is more than just reading a few verses from the Bible in the morning and trying to be a good person that day. Seeking requires me to sacrifice the things I feel compelled to chase so I can be available to notice God's clear direction.

Whatever we chase, like it or not, gains our full attention.

And I wonder sometimes why I feel a little insecure—a little unsettled—a little disappointed with things I thought would make me so happy. I guess you could say sometimes I get a little homesick.

While I love vacationing here in this world for however many years the Lord will give me, I know where my real home is, and I know who is waiting for me there.

And now I know He takes time to tie up little care packages from home—a few things I need, a few things I'm supposed to pass on to others, and a few things He knows will simply bring me joy.

Then God waits . . . to see . . . if I'll notice—if I'll remember . . . if today will be the day . . . that I lift up my face . . . pause in the busyness . . . and really seek Him above all else.

Dear Lord, forgive me for all the times I've rushed by Your gifts and overlooked Your blessings. Today, I want to pause and really seek You with all I've got. I love You, Lord. In Jesus' Name, Amen.

33

WHERE BROKENNESS RUNS DEEP

LORD, you alone are my portion and my cup;
  you make my lot secure.
The boundary lines have fallen for me in
  pleasant places;
  surely I have a delightful inheritance.
  —PSALM 16:5–6

Our sweet little dog, Chelsea, is not the brightest bulb in the lamp around cars driving down our long driveway. Though she has plenty of room to run and play inside our fenced-in yard, she is obsessed with trying to attack the tires crunching against our gravel drive whenever someone drives on our property. As a result, she had an unfortunate encounter with a moving vehicle one day.

I wept like a baby when I saw her. But, other than a broken front leg, a severely scraped-up back leg, and a nose with half the flesh missing, she fared okay. Mercy.

The vet informed us that in order for her leg to properly heal, we'd have to keep her calm for three weeks. Yikes. It would be a challenge to keep Chelsea still for three minutes. But three weeks? That seemed impossible!

Well, two weeks into the healing journey all that stillness got the best of sweet Chelsea in the middle of the night. She decided she would punish me with a fit of whining, crying, and banging my closed bathroom door. She wanted out and she wanted out now. She wanted to run and chase some unsuspecting night creature. The temptation was too strong and she was sick of sacrificing her freedom.

To be honest, I wanted her to be able to run and chase a night creature too. But my love for this dog would not permit me to allow her to harm herself. Her brokenness couldn't handle that kind of freedom.

Not yet.

As I tossed and turned in the wee hours of the morning, that statement about Chelsea's brokenness struck me as quite applicable to myself as well. How often do I find myself in situations where my brokenness can't handle freedom outside the boundaries God has set for me?

I was made to be a victorious child of God.

Sometimes we need boundaries around our own unique struggles and temptations. Food. Screen time. Shopping. A certain relationship. God helps us put boundaries in place, knowing that we need more time to heal before we can step outside of them. Honoring those boundaries helps strengthen us and move us forward in our healing. Here are a few things I try to remind myself when I find myself like Chelsea—upset, crying, and trying to step out beyond what God wants for me in that moment:

- I am not made to be a victim of my poor choices. I was made to be a victorious child of God.
- When I am struggling and considering a compromise, I will force myself to think past this moment and ask myself, *How will I feel about this choice tomorrow morning?*

- If I am in a situation where the temptation is overwhelming, I will have to choose to either remove the temptation or remove myself from the situation.
- I have these boundaries in place not for restriction but to define the parameters of my freedom. Psalm 16:6 reminds me that the boundary lines God has placed in my life are in good and pleasant places. My brokenness can't handle more freedom than this right now. And I'm good with that.

This battle is hard. Really hard. It can feel like a war is being waged in your head.

It breaks my heart that so many of God's girls feel powerless in their struggles. But we can band together, get honest, grab hold of the truths that will set us free, and do something about it.

One of my own greatest struggles has been in the area of food. It's what some of the following devotions will be about. But I don't want you to skim over them if food isn't your struggle. I am praying you will take the truths I share and apply them to your own battles. Your own personal areas of weakness and temptation that the Lord has been stirring your heart to believe you can overcome.

Yes, victory is possible, sisters, not by figuring out how to make this an easy process, but by choosing—over and over and over and over again—the absolute power available through God's truth.

Dear Lord, You know where my brokenness runs deep. Please help me to set some healthy boundaries and to heal. In Jesus' Name, Amen.

34

CONSUMED BY CRAVINGS

How lovely is your dwelling place,
   LORD Almighty!
My soul yearns, even faints,
   for the courts of the LORD;
my heart and my flesh cry out
   for the living God.

—PSALM 84:1–2

A few years ago, a weight-loss company came up with a brilliant advertising campaign. Maybe you saw some of their ads. A little orange monster chases a woman around, tempting and taunting her with foods that obviously aren't a part of her healthy eating plan. The ads perfectly capture what it feels like to be harassed by cravings all day long.

While I've never seen this orange monster chasing me, I've felt its presence. I've felt it for food cravings, but I know that we all feel it for something. Sometimes, many somethings.

Attention and satisfaction. *Like me.* Approval and appreciation. *Follow me.* Money and power. *Give me.* More, more, more. Sometimes it feels like the chase will never end, the cravings will never be filled . . . that nothing will ever be enough.

While the orange monster is a great way to visualize cravings, those ads fell short in their promise to really help a woman. The weight-loss company's theory is to teach what foods are more filling and encourage consumption of those. But does that really help overcome cravings?

> *We were made to crave—long for, want greatly, desire eagerly, and beg for—God. Only God.*

We shop and spend money on things we don't need. We still eat the chocolate pie when we're full from our dinner. We scroll through social media, checking our pages and counting our likes and comments. We indulge in our guilty pleasures, hide our secret sins, and lie in bed wondering if this is it. *Is this it?*

What is actually going on here?

I believe God made us to crave. Now before you think this is some sort of cruel joke by God, let me assure you that the object of our craving was never supposed to be food or the many other things people find themselves consumed by.

Think about the definition of the word *craving*. How would you define it? Dictionary.com defines *craving* as something you long for, want greatly, desire eagerly, and beg for. Now consider this expression of craving: "How lovely is your dwelling place, Lord Almighty! My soul yearns, even faints, for the courts of the Lord; my heart and my flesh cry out for the living God" (Psalm 84:1–2).

Yes, we were made to crave—long for, want greatly, desire eagerly, and beg for—God. Only God.

Sweet sister, does this resonate with you?

Have you chosen to pursue God, to follow Jesus? He created you to know Him, to be fulfilled more deeply by knowing Him than by any other experience or pleasure this world has to offer. When we admit our need for Him, when we humble ourselves and confess our sins and ask Him to be Lord of our lives, that's where the journey begins. He saves us in that moment, and then we can begin the process of allowing Him to fulfill our cravings and make us eternally, completely, and wholly filled.

Is it easy?

No.

Is it worth it?

A thousand times *yes*.

Dear God, I am an imperfect person, a sinner, and I need You. Please forgive me for giving in to cravings that will never satisfy. I want to follow You. In Jesus' Name, Amen.

35

PHYSICALLY OVERWEIGHT AND SPIRITUALLY UNDERWEIGHT

"My food," said Jesus, "is to do the will of him who sent me and to finish his work."

—JOHN 4:34

If you've attended many Christian women's events, you've probably heard the story of the Samaritan woman told from just about every possible angle. If I hear someone start to speak about her at a conference, I'll admit my brain begs me to tune out and daydream about tropical places or items I need to add to my grocery list.

It's not that I don't like her story. I do. It's just that I've heard it so many times I find myself doubting there could possibly be anything fresh left to say about it. But in all my years of hearing about the Samaritan woman, reading her story, and feeling like I know it, I missed something. Something really big.

Right smack-dab in the middle of one of the longest recorded interactions Jesus has with a woman, He starts talking about food. Food! And I'd never picked up on it before. I somehow missed Jesus' crucial teaching that our bodies must have two kinds of nourishment: physical and spiritual.

Just as I must have physical food for my body to survive, I need spiritual food for my soul to thrive. Jesus says, "My food . . . is to do the will of him who sent me and to finish his work" (John 4:34). And then He goes on to say, "I tell you, open your eyes and look at the fields! They are ripe for harvest" (John 4:35).

In the midst of offering salvation to the Samaritan woman, Jesus seems to wander off on this tangent about food. But it's not a tangent at all.

Actually, it fits perfectly. It relates directly to the core issue of spiritual malnutrition. Specifically, it's about trying to use food to fill not only the physical void of our stomachs but also the spiritual void of our souls. For years, I was physically overweight but spiritually underweight.

Jesus wants us to know only He can fill us and truly satisfy us.

As I mentioned before, I realize food may not be your area of struggle. But I believe we all have things in our lives that we are tempted to turn to instead of Jesus to fill the aching places in our souls. How crucial it is for us to remember:

Food can fill our stomachs but never our souls.

Possessions can fill our houses but never our hearts.

Children can fill our days but never our identities.

Jesus wants us to know only He can fill us and truly satisfy us. He really wants us to believe that with all of our hearts.

Only by being filled with authentic soul food from Jesus—following Him and telling others about Him—will our souls ever be truly satisfied. And breaking free from whatever consumes our thoughts more than Jesus allows us to see and pursue our callings with more confidence and clarity.

Dear Lord, I know that it is true that only You can fill me. I acknowledge that You are the Lord of my life. I want to please You today in all that I do. Help me follow You. In Jesus' Name, Amen.

36

An Undivided Heart

*My flesh and my heart may fail, but God is the
strength of my heart and my portion forever.*
—Psalm 73:26

knew my weight issue didn't have anything to do with me being
spiritual or worldly. If I was honest with myself, my issue was plain
and simple—a lack of self-control. I could sugarcoat it and justify it
all day long, but the truth was I didn't have a weight problem; I had
a spiritual problem. I depended on food for comfort more than I
depended on God. And I was simply too lazy to make time to exercise.

Ouch. That truth hurt.

So, one day a couple of years ago, I got up first thing in the morning and went running. And you know what? I hated it. Exercise just
made me want to cry.

It made me hot and sticky. It made my legs hurt and my lungs
burn. Nothing about it was fun until after I finished. But the feeling
of accomplishment I felt afterward was fantastic! So each day I would
fight through the tears and excuses and make the effort to run.

At first I could only slowly jog from one mailbox to another—in
a neighborhood where the houses are close together, thank you very
much. Slowly, I started to see little evidences of progress. Every day I
asked God to give me the strength to stick with it this time. I'd tried so
many other times and failed. The more I made running about spiritual

growth and discipline, the less I focused on the weight. Each lost pound was not a quest to get skinny but evidence of obedience to God.

One day, I went out for my run and a clear command from God rumbled in my heart: "Run until you can't take another step. Do it not in your strength but in Mine. Every time you want to stop, pray—and don't stop until I tell you to."

I had a record up to that point of running three miles, which I thought was quite stellar. So maybe God wanted me to run just slightly past the three-mile marker and rejoice in relying on His strength to do so. But as I reached that point in my run, my heart betrayed my aching body and said, "Keep going."

Each step thereafter, I had to pray and rely on God. The more I focused on running toward God, the less I thought about my desire to stop. And this verse from the Psalms came to life: "My flesh and my heart may fail, but God is the strength of my heart and my portion forever" (73:26).

As I ran that day, I connected with God on a different level. I experienced what it meant to absolutely require God's faith to see something through. How many times have I claimed to be a woman of faith but rarely lived a life requiring faith? That day, God didn't have me stop until I ran 8.6 miles.

Hear me out here. It was *my* legs that took every step. It was *my* energy being used. It was *my* effort that took me from one mile to three to five to seven to 8.6. But it was *God's strength* replacing my excuses step by step by step.

> How many times have I claimed to be a woman of faith but rarely lived a life requiring faith?

For a mailbox-to-mailbox, crying-when-she-thought-of-exercising, allergic-to-physical-discipline kind of girl, it was a modern-day miracle. I broke through the "I can't" barrier and expanded the horizons of my reality. Was it hard? Yes. Was it tempting to quit? Absolutely. Could I do this in my own strength? Never. But this really wasn't about running. It was about realizing the power of God taking over my complete weakness.

I went back to my standard three-mile track the next time I ran. But slowly I increased my daily runs to four miles and am very happy with that distance. Running 8.6 miles on a daily basis isn't realistic for me. But that one day, it was glorious. Especially because of what I discovered when I got home.

Since I'd been thinking of a verse from Psalms during my run, I grabbed my Bible as soon as I got home and opened it up to Psalm 86, in honor of my 8.6 miles.

Here is part of what I read: "Teach me your way, LORD, that I may rely on your faithfulness; give me an undivided heart, that I may fear your name. I will praise you, Lord my God, with all my heart; I will glorify your name forever" (Psalm 86:11–12).

An undivided heart. That's what my whole journey in conquering my cravings was about. When it comes to my body, I can't live with divided loyalties. I can either be loyal to honoring the Lord with my body or loyal to my cravings, desires, and many excuses for not exercising.

I don't know where you might have divided loyalties or what struggle makes you think, *I can't*. But are you open to God's leading in how He wants to show His power in your life?

Dear Lord, I want to have a heart that is totally loyal to You. Please show me if there are things I turn to instead of You. Teach me to rely on Your strength and power in the areas where I am weak. In Jesus' Name, Amen.

SHOCKED BY MY OWN ADVICE

"Enter through the narrow gate. For wide is the gate
and broad is the road that leads to destruction, and
many enter through it. But small is the gate and narrow
the road that leads to life, and only a few find it."

—MATTHEW 7:13–14

Today's key verses are not easy for a girl who wanted nothing more growing up than to fit in. Don't cause waves. Don't stand out. Don't stand up. Don't rock the boat of norm in any way. Just go with the flow in the same direction as everyone else.

But somewhere along my Christian journey, going with the flow started to bother me.

Verses like the one above in Matthew 7 and Romans 12:2, "Do not conform any longer to the pattern of this world, but be transformed by the renewing of your mind," started to mess with my status-quo existence.

Conformed or transformed? The choice is mine. If I want to be a sold-out somebody for God, I have to break away from the everybody crowd.

This is a message I shared with my son several years ago when he came to me scared. He admitted things had gone a little too far with his girlfriend and wanted help processing what to do. They hadn't crossed every line but enough that he knew they were headed in a dangerous direction.

We sat on the back deck and processed the situation together. We read a list of empowering Scripture verses seeking to filter every part of this situation through God's truth. In the end, he and his girlfriend came to the realization they needed to break up. It's really hard to put things in reverse after certain lines have been crossed.

I walked back into the house after that conversation with two things running through my brain. I was thrilled my son came to me to talk about such a sensitive issue. What an honor to breathe Truth into his physical struggle.

Conformed or transformed? The choice is mine. If I want to be a sold-out somebody for God, I have to break away from the everybody crowd.

But I was also feeling a little panicked at the realities of parenting older teenagers. And that feeling led me straight to the pantry, convinced I *needed* some chocolate. I *deserved* some chips! As I loaded my arms full of treats, I was suddenly struck by a gut-wrenching question. How could I expect my son to apply Truth to his area of physical struggle but refuse to apply it to my area of physical struggle with food?

Ouch. I was shocked by my own advice.

If I wanted to model what it looks like to live out truth in my physical struggles, I would have to break up with unhealthy choices. God made me to consume food, but food was never supposed to consume me.

Making healthy choices with my food would have to be part of my breaking away. I would have to distance myself from my distraction if I wanted to become truly transformed.

What's your distraction? What's the one way you can start to break away from the everybody crowd?

The everybody crowd says, "If it feels good it is good." The everybody crowd says, "Don't deny yourself . . . that's so old-school." The everybody crowd says, "Everybody's living it up—so should you." Conformed or transformed? The choice is ours. If we want to be sold-out for God, we have to break away from the everybody crowd.

Dear Lord, I want and need to live apart from the everybody crowd. Free me of my distractions. Remove my insecurities. Help me to follow You with my whole heart. In Jesus' Name, Amen.

38

THE VALUE OF EMPTINESS

He said to me, "My grace is sufficient for you, for
my power is made perfect in weakness." Therefore I
will boast all the more gladly about my weaknesses,
so that Christ's power may rest on me.

—2 CORINTHIANS 12:9

once had a fascinating discussion about discipline with three
pastors. The question was thrown out, "Is discipline really sustain-
able?" One chuckled as he stuffed a second yeast roll in his mouth and
said, "Obviously, not for me."

The second leaned back in his chair and expressed his doubt
as well.

The third piped in with an absolute yes and gave biblical support
for his emphatic answer.

I never got to give my answer that day. We had a tight schedule
and our conversation turned to other matters. But if I had been able
to give my answer, it would have been this: no and yes.

No, I do not believe in our own strength we can sustain a level of
discipline that requires real sacrifice for a long period of time.

However, my answer is yes when you factor in a crucial spiritual
truth. Making the connection between my daily disciplines and my
desire to pursue holiness is crucial. Holiness doesn't just deal with

my spiritual life; it deals with every single part of my life. My body. My mind. My relationships. My time.

It is good for God's people to be put in a place of longing so they feel a slight desperation. Only then can we be empty enough and open enough to discover the holiness we were made for. When we are stuffed full of other things and never allow ourselves to be in a place of longing, we don't recognize the deeper spiritual battle going on.

> *The more dependent we become on God's strength, the less enamored we will be with other choices.*

Satan wants to keep us distracted by making us chase one temporary filling after another. God wants us to step back and let the emptying process have its way until we start desiring a holier approach to life. The gap between our frail discipline and God's available strength is bridged with nothing but a simple choice on our part to pursue this holiness.

Moment by moment we have the choice to live in our own strength and risk failure or to reach across the gap and grab hold of God's unwavering strength. He promises us in 2 Corinthians 12:9 that His grace will be sufficient for us—even in our areas of greatest weakness. And the beautiful thing is, the more dependent we become on God's strength, the less enamored we will be with other choices.

Dear Lord, I am weak. Please help me pause and feel the emptiness and longing deep within. I want to live by Your holiness and strength. In Jesus' Name, Amen.

39

SATAN'S PLAN AGAINST YOU

Everything in the world—the lust of the flesh,
the lust of the eyes, and the pride of life—comes
not from the Father but from the world.

—1 JOHN 2:16

*S*omething I pray on a regular basis is that God will give me a keen awareness of the Enemy's plans and schemes against me. I want to be able to recognize his traps and avoid them.

I believe part of His answer came one day as I studied the story of Satan tempting Eve in Genesis 3 and our key verse: "Everything in the world—the lust of the flesh, the lust of the eyes, and the pride of life—comes not from the Father but from the world" (1 John 2:16).

As I compared these passages, I had a serious epiphany about how Satan goes after us. These verses outline Satan's three-pronged plan of attack on our hearts. And it's the same plan we see him using while tempting Jesus in the desert in Matthew 4:1–11! A fact that tells me while the Enemy may be powerful, he's also predictable.

Let's take a closer look at Satan's plan as revealed in Eve's story and Jesus' story:

1. Make them crave some sort of physical gratification to the point they become preoccupied with it, be it sex, drugs, alcohol, or food. Satan tempted Eve with fruit, which "was good for food" (Genesis 3:6).

Satan tempted Jesus while the Lord was on a fast with bread.

Satan tempts us with whatever physical stimulation we are too preoccupied by—be it taste, smell, sound, touch, or sight. These things are good within the boundaries where God meant for them to be enjoyed. But venture outside God's intention for them, and they become an attempt to try and get our needs met outside the will of God.

Satan's power over us is nothing compared to the freeing promises of God.

2. Make them want to acquire things to the point they bow down to the god of materialism. Keep them distracted by making their eyes lust after the shiny things of the world. Satan tempted Eve by drawing her attention to what was "pleasing to the eye" (Genesis 3:6).

Satan showed Jesus the kingdoms of the world and told Him that He could have it all.

Satan flashes the newer, bigger, and seemingly better things of this world in front of us, trying to lure us into thinking we must have it. *This will make me fulfilled. This will make me happy.* And then it wears out, breaks down, gets old, and reveals just how temporary every material thing is.

3. Make them boastful about what they have or do. Keep them distracted and obsessed with their status and significance. Choke the life out of them using the tentacles of their own pride. Satan tempted Eve by promising an increased awareness that would make her become more like God.

Satan tempted Jesus by telling Him to throw Himself off the highest point of the temple, and then command the angels to save Him.

This would impress everyone watching and certainly raise Jesus' status and significance.

Likewise, Satan tempts us to try and elevate ourselves over others. We wrongly think we have to become something the world calls worthy. This creates a need within our flesh to have people notice us, commend us, revere us, and stroke our pride. We then dare to boast about all we are.

Oh, sweet sisters, this is where we must stop and remind ourselves that we don't have to be held hostage by Satan. We are onto him and his schemes. And his power over us is nothing compared to the freeing promises of God.

There was a huge difference between Eve's response to Satan and Jesus' response to Satan. Eve dialoged with Satan and allowed him to weave his tangled web of justifications. Jesus, on the other hand, immediately quoted truth. With every temptation, Jesus quoted Deuteronomy as He answered, "It is written . . ." and He shut Satan down with the truth of God.

What will our response be?

It's our choice.

Moment by moment, decision by decision, step by step—will we operate in God's all-powerful truth or allow Satan to entangle us in his lies?

Dear Lord, thank You for making me aware of the Enemy's plans against me. I declare today that while the Enemy may be vicious, he will not be victorious in my life. Not with You helping me walk in Truth and Light. In Jesus' Name, Amen.

40

When the End Goal Seems Too Hard

Make every effort to add to your faith goodness;
and to goodness, knowledge; and to knowledge,
self-control; and to self-control, perseverance.

—2 Peter 1:5–6

*N*o matter what your struggle has been, victory is possible today. Sadly, most of us don't think that's true. The problem is, we tend to measure long-term success while downplaying the absolute victory found in small successes.

Recently a friend of mine called to say she walked away from an impulse buy online. That's a victorious small success. Now, I can't say that her bank account will stand up and clap and reward her with a much higher balance. But, if she builds upon this small success—choice by choice, day by day—she will see positive changes.

This principle applies to other struggles as well.

If I choose not to snap at a loved one and instead respond with tenderness, that's a victorious small success.

If I choose to pause before responding to the rude sales clerk, thus giving her a smile instead of perpetuating her smirk, that's a victorious small success.

I like the way 2 Peter 1:5–6 puts it. We are reminded to "add" some things to our faith. Two of those additions are self-control and

Big things are built one brick at a time. Victories are achieved one choice at a time. A life well lived is chosen one day at a time.

perseverance. For me, I have to decide to practice the self-control and perseverance that are mine since God's Spirit lives in me.

Think of it like a muscle. We have muscles as a part of our bodies. But we must add activity to those muscles to make them effective and strong. Our muscles will work for us if we exercise them. Self-control and perseverance will work for us as we practice them over and over. Start with the small victories and bigger victories will come.

Sometimes victory seems so far away because we measure it by the end goal. And end goals can seem overwhelmingly huge, daunting, and just plain hard to reach. Instead, if we start measuring our victories by the smaller choices we make each day, victory won't seem so impossible.

Big things are built one brick at a time.

Victories are achieved one choice at a time.

A life well lived is chosen one day at a time.

Dear Lord, I know that with You, victory is indeed possible. Day by day and choice by choice. Help me believe this truth today. In Jesus' Name, Amen.

41

Replacing Old Lies with New Truths

I am convinced that neither death nor life, neither
angels nor demons, neither the present nor the future,
nor any powers, neither height nor depth, nor anything
else in all creation, will be able to separate us from
the love of God that is in Christ Jesus our Lord.

—Romans 8:38–39

had been going through some rotten, horrible, no-good days and was at the absolute end of knowing what to pray. I'd slipped into a habit of praying circumstance-oriented prayers where I'd list out every problem and ask God to please fix them. I even made suggestions for solutions in case my input could be useful. But nothing changed.

In a huff one day, I sat down to pray and had absolutely no words. None. I sat there staring blankly. I had no suggestions. I had no solutions. I had nothing but quiet tears. But eventually, God broke through to my worn-out heart. A thought rushed through my mind and caught me off guard. *I know you want Me to change your circumstances, Lysa. But, right now I want to focus on changing you. Even perfect circumstances won't satisfy you like letting Me change the way you think.*

I didn't like what I heard during this first time of silently sitting with the Lord, but at least I felt I was connecting with God. I hadn't felt that in a long time. And so I started making it a habit to sit quietly before the Lord.

Sometimes I cried. Sometimes I sat with a bad attitude. Sometimes I sat with a heart so heavy I wasn't sure I'd be able to carry on much longer. But as I sat, I pictured God sitting there with me. He was there already and I eventually sensed that. I experienced what the apostle Paul taught when he wrote, "In the same way, the Spirit helps us in our weakness. We do not know what we ought to pray for, but the Spirit himself intercedes for us with groans that words cannot express" (Romans 8:26).

If we are really going to make progress toward lasting changes, we have to empty ourselves of the lie that other people or things can ever fill our hearts to the full.

As I sat in silence, the Spirit interceded with perfect prayers on my behalf. I didn't have to figure out *what* to pray or *how* to pray about this situation that seemed so consuming. I just had to be still and sit with the Lord. And during those sitting times, I started to discern changes I needed to make in response to my circumstances.

If we are really going to make progress toward lasting change in our lives, we have to empty ourselves of the lie that other people or things can ever fill our hearts to the full. Then we have to deliberately and intentionally fill up on God's truths and stand secure in His love.

I have to mentally replace the lies using some of my favorite verses to remind myself of just how filling God's love really is. Here's one that really helps me:

> For I am convinced that neither death nor life, neither angels nor demons, neither the present nor the future, nor any powers, neither height nor depth, nor anything else in all creation, will be able to separate us from the love of God that is in Christ Jesus our Lord. (Romans 8:38–39)

We'll talk more about this in tomorrow's devotion, but for now I want to encourage you to think on some of your favorite verses and write out some old lies and new truths on your own. Sweet friend, the process of stripping away old lies is hard and can produce raw feelings. That's why it's so crucial to have truths with which to replace them.

Dear Lord, please help me to recognize the lies I need to let go of. I want to fill up on Your truth instead. In Jesus' Name, Amen.

42

TURNING NORTH

The LORD said to me, "You have made your way around
this hill country long enough; now turn north."
—DEUTERONOMY 2:2–3

We all have messes in our lives. Financial messes. Relationship messes. Health messes. Kid messes. Home messes. Business messes. Messes that leave us feeling stuck. Like we may be stranded in this place of upheaval and unrest forever.

I can't help but think about the people of Israel as they were wandering through the desert. We read in the book of Deuteronomy about how they were stuck in a mess with no end in sight. God had miraculously set them free from the oppression and bondage of slavery in Egypt. But their unwillingness to fully trust Him and their blatant refusal to take possession of the promised land landed them in quite a mess. A forty-year, desert-wandering mess.

In Deuteronomy 2, Moses reminds them of a time when they had been stuck circling the same mountain for too long. God spoke into their wandering and let them know it was time to head in a new direction.

The LORD said to me, "You have made your way around this hill country long enough; now turn north." (Deuteronomy 2:2–3)

It was a pivotal moment for them to remember. One where they had faced a life-changing choice. They could stay stuck, endlessly circling the same old place, or they could choose hope and head in a new direction with the Lord.

Am I letting this mess define me or refine me?

They could turn north.

I think this is the perfect time to pause and ask God if there is anywhere we need to "turn north" in our own lives. Have we been circling the same messes for years and years with no end in sight? Are there areas we know we need to change but we feel like it will require too much sacrifice?

Here's a question we can ask ourselves right in the midst of our messes . . .

Am I letting this mess *define* me or *refine* me?

The answer to this question is crucial.

If I am letting a mess *define* me, I will feel *hopeless*.

If I am letting a mess *refine* me, I will be *hopeful*.

If the Israelites had looked at their forty-year track record of aimless wandering and defined themselves as rebellious failures, they would have lost all hope and kept right on circling. But because they embraced the correction and redirection of the Lord, they were able to turn around and move toward His promises with hope firmly planted in their hearts.

It's time for our messes to stop defining us.

It's time to embrace the refining process and turn north.

So how do we begin to turn north? We replace our old thoughts with empowering truths from God's Word, just like we talked about yesterday. I call them "Go-To Scripts." In other words, these statements can become our new patterns of thought. And these new patterns of thought will empower us for a new way of living.

Here are some of my favorite "Go-To Scripts" for turning north:

1. I was made for more than to be stuck in a vicious cycle of defeat. Deuteronomy 2:3, "You have made your way around this hill country long enough; now turn north."

2. When tempted, I either remove the temptation or remove myself from the situation. 1 Corinthians 10:13–14, "God is faithful; he will not let you be tempted beyond what you can bear. But when you are tempted, he will also provide a way out so that you can endure it. Therefore, my dear friends, flee."

3. I don't have to worry about letting God down, because I was never holding Him up—God's grace is sufficient. 2 Corinthians 12:9–11, "He said to me, 'My grace is sufficient for you, for my power is made perfect in weakness . . . for when I am weak, then I am strong.'"

May we hear the Father's voice, filled with grace and free from any hint of condemnation, declaring over us today, "It's time to turn north, beloved." And may we be found turning toward Him and moving forward with Him.

Dear Lord, thank You for looking on me with love and continually offering me hope. I'm choosing to believe today that I don't have to stay stuck in my messes. I'm tuning my ear to Your voice today. I'm filling my heart and mind with the truth of Your Word. And I'm heading in a new direction with You. In Jesus' Name, Amen.

43

How Much Will This Choice Really Cost Me?

In order that Satan might not outwit us. For
we are not unaware of his schemes.
—2 Corinthians 2:11

A few years ago I sat at the Department of Motor Vehicles (DMV) with one of my daughters while an officer told her the importance of good choices. She was getting her learner's permit and entering the scary world of teenage drivers.

"We've had 320 teens killed this year in fatal car accidents, so we want to do everything possible to keep you safe," the officer said sternly as she highlighted for my daughter all the many rules for new drivers. Then she suggested signing a contract with her parents incorporating these rules.

I've never wanted to hug a DMV officer. But it was all I could do not to reach across the desk and throw my arms around her. For, you see, I had already created a driving contract that each of my teenagers had to sign.

I'm sure the kids thought the contract was a bit over the top. After all, none of their friends had to sign such a document with their parents. So it was good to hear another adult speak truth into the life of my child.

And what I loved most about the officer's sermonette on safe driving was her emphasis on the cost of wrong choices.

If I know how much something is going to cost me, I make much wiser choices.

How I wish we could all see the cost of our choices as clearly as a price tag on items in a store. If I know how much something is going to cost me, I make much wiser choices. But we have an Enemy who schemes against us to keep the cost of dumb decisions concealed until it's too late.

Satan wants to defeat, discourage, and destroy our families. His attacks are not just willy-nilly attempts to trip us up or knock us down. He wants to take us out.

Do you know why Satan's tactics are called schemes in 2 Corinthians 2:11? A scheme is a plan, design, or program of action. Satan's schemes are well-crafted plans specifically targeted to increase your desire for something outside the will of God, make you think giving in to a weakness is no big deal, and minimize your ability to think through the consequences of falling for this temptation.

Satan is a master of keeping that cost hidden until it's too late.

Sweet sisters, this is something worth thinking about. And it's something worth talking about with our kids and the people we love. Consider age-appropriate examples of how costly wrong choices can be. Be real, raw, and bold as you walk them through different scenarios of temptations they might face.

That DMV officer was certainly bold in her explanation of the cost when a teen driver gets distracted by their cell phone or friends acting silly. Hearing her explain to my daughter how costly others' poor choices have been made these "rules" seem more like life-saving gifts.

Think how different life might be if we all paused and asked ourselves this crucial question: *How much will this choice really cost me?* If we teach ourselves and those entrusted to us nothing else this week than to ask this one question, we will have invested wisely. So, so very wisely.

Dear Lord, I am reminded that boldly following You is so much better than any short-term experience that's not pleasing to You. Give me Your eyes so I can see temptation and its many different faces. In Jesus' Name, Amen.

44

THE COURAGEOUS CHOICE

I eagerly expect and hope that I will in no way be ashamed,
but will have sufficient courage so that now as always Christ
will be exalted in my body, whether by life or by death.
—PHILIPPIANS 1:20

One day, I had the most interesting conversation with a friend who lives in Hollywood. Although her family lives in the middle of glitz, glamour, and extreme excess, she said they are determined to teach their kids something rare—the courageous choice.

You see, there are two kinds of courage. There's the courageous act that makes our hearts beat fast when the knight fights the dragon or the firefighter rushes into the burning building. These are extreme events many of us won't have to face. And because most of us aren't put in positions to participate in a courageous act, we don't necessarily think of ourselves as courageous.

But there's a second kind of courage that is widely available but not widely embraced. It's the *courageous choice.* This is the decision to do the right thing even when it's unpopular, uncelebrated, and probably even unnoticed.

Have you been faced with one of these kinds of choices lately? Probably one of my toughest courageous choices has been in the area of my food choices. It was my hidden struggle. The one I didn't want to deal with or talk about. Not with my friends and certainly not with God.

But then I started coming across verse after verse in the Bible that spoke directly to my issue. Though I didn't want to talk to God about it, God certainly seemed to want to speak to me. Verses like Philippians 1:20: "I eagerly expect and hope that I will in no way be ashamed, but will have sufficient courage so that now as always Christ will be exalted in my body, whether by life or by death."

It is possible to layer one courageous choice upon another and find victory in your area of struggle.

He also spoke to me through Psalm 73:26: "My flesh and my heart may fail, but God is the strength of my heart and my portion forever." And 2 Corinthians 7:1: "Since we have these promises, dear friends, let us purify ourselves from everything that contaminates body and spirit, perfecting holiness out of reverence for God."

God assured me He loved me exactly how I was, but He loved me too much to leave me in a state of defeat.

I made a courageous choice to read the Bible looking for God to speak to me about my struggle. I made the courageous choice to walk willingly on the path of discipline. I made the courageous choice to pick something healthy even in the quietness of my pantry when no one else was looking.

I made the courageous choice to put a stake in the ground and say to myself, *I'm more than the sum total of my screaming taste buds. My heart doesn't want that junk food. My arms don't want that junk food.*

My legs don't want that junk food. And my soul certainly doesn't want that junk food.

It is possible to layer one courageous choice upon another and find victory in your area of struggle. No matter what your struggle is, are you willing to make one courageous choice today?

Make that choice.

And then make it again.

And then make it again.

You are a courageous woman. Now, go out and prove it to yourself.

Dear Lord, I acknowledge that I need Your divine help with each choice I make every day. I don't ever want to step outside Your will and direction for my life. I am courageous only with You, in You, and through You. Please help me embrace Your courageous choices for me. In Jesus' Name, Amen.

45

TELLING MY FLESH NO

I pray that you, being rooted and established in love, may
have power, together with all the Lord's holy people, to grasp
how wide and long and high and deep is the love of Christ.

—EPHESIANS 3:17–18

I don't like to be in pain. In any way. And if I'm not careful, this aversion to pain can lead to me grabbing at anyone and anything to fill the deep ache in my soul.

Maybe you can relate.

When you're lonely and you see your friends post a picture together at a gathering you weren't invited to—your flesh will want to grab at something. It's hard not to comfort yourself by venting all your frustrations to another friend or family member.

When you're listening to other moms talk about all the progress their children are making in reading and your child can't even identify letters yet, your flesh will want to grab at something. It's hard not to throw out a statement to one-up the bragging moms in an area where your child is excelling.

And all these things we're tempted to grab at? They won't fill us the way we think they will. In the end, they only make us feel emptier. But how do we tell our flesh no when we are desperate for relief?

I have discovered that the more we fill ourselves from God's life-giving love, the less we will be dictated by the grabby-ness of our flesh.

One of the most beautiful descriptions of the fullness of God is found in Paul's prayer for the Ephesians:

For this reason I kneel before the Father, from whom every family in heaven and on earth derives its name. I pray that out of his glorious riches he may strengthen you with power through his Spirit in your inner being, so that Christ may dwell in your hearts through faith. And I pray that you, being rooted and established in love, may have power, together with all the Lord's holy people, to grasp how wide and long and high and deep is the love of Christ, and to know this love that surpasses knowledge—that you may be filled to the measure of all the fullness of God. (Ephesians 3:14–19)

My favorite part of Paul's prayer is him asking that we will have the power to grasp the fullness of the love of Christ . . . for then we will be filled with the fullness of God.

If we grasp the full love of Christ, we won't grab at other things to fill us. Or if we do, we'll sense it. We'll feel a prick in our spirits when our flesh makes frenzied swipes at happiness, and we'll pause.

In this pause lies the greatest daily choice we can make. *Am I willing to tell my flesh no, so I can say yes to the fullness of God in this situation?*

And this isn't about us putting on a brave face and hoping for the best when we feel powerless. We have the power through Christ, who is over every power, including the pull of the flesh. When we have Christ, we are full—fully loved and accepted and empowered to say no.

This is true on the days we feel it, and it's still true when we don't feel Jesus' love at all. If we live rooted and established in His love, we don't just have knowledge of His love in our minds, but it becomes a reality that anchors us. Though winds of hurt blow, they cannot uproot us and rip us apart. His love holds us. His love grounds us. His love is a glorious weight preventing

If we grasp the full love of Christ, we won't grab at other things to fill us.

harsh words and hurtful situations from being a destructive force. We feel the wind but aren't destroyed by it. This is the "fullness of God."

There is power in really knowing this. This isn't dependent on what you've accomplished. Or on another person loving you or accepting you. Nor is it because you always feel full. You are full, because Christ brought the fullness to you.

Yes, I am fully loved, fully accepted, and fully empowered to say no to my flesh. Speak that truth in the power He's given you. Believe that truth in the power He's given you. Live that truth in the power He's given you.

That's how we tell our flesh no. That's how we live fully prepared in the fullness of God.

Father God, thank You for Your love for me that knows no end. Help me look to You and You alone to fill me. I want my roots to go down ever deeper in Your love. In Jesus' Name, Amen.

Why Do I Have So Many Issues?

There is now no condemnation for
those who are in Christ Jesus.
—ROMANS 8:1

*H*ave you ever looked at other people and thought to yourself, *How does everyone else have it all together? And why is it that I seem to have so many issues?*

I understand. As you have already read in the previous devotions, I've struggled with my weight and committing to a healthy lifestyle most of my life. My soul was rubbed raw from years of trying and failing.

I wanted something to instantly fix my issues.

I wanted to stop calling myself awful names I'd never let another person call me.

I wanted to be naturally thin like my sister.

I wanted to stop crying when I walked into my closet to get dressed in the morning.

So when I lost twenty-five pounds a few years ago and kept it off for the first time in my life, it was a huge victory.

But my real celebration hasn't been over the smaller clothing size and reduced numbers on the scale. My real celebration is over the spiritual insights I gained while losing the weight and maintaining my healthy progress.

For me, this has been a spiritual journey—a significant spiritual journey with great physical benefits. I had been overweight physically and underweight spiritually, and finally tying those two things together was life changing.

How dangerous it is to hold up the intimate knowledge of our imperfections against the outside packaging of others.

One of the richest lessons has been realizing the amount of mental and spiritual energy I wasted for years just wishing things would change. All the while, I was beating myself up for not having the discipline to make those changes.

If you have an issue with weight and food, you know what I mean. But no matter what issue you are currently dealing with, can I offer a bit of encouragement?

Jesus wants to help you with that issue. He really does. But you've got to stop beating yourself up about it and determine to follow His lead.

We like to identify our shortcomings, form them into a club, and beat the tar out of ourselves mentally. Over and over and over again. We label ourselves and soon lose our real identity to the beaten and bruised fragility we call "me."

We compare, we assume, we assess, we measure, and most times walk away shaking our heads at how woefully short our "me" falls compared to everyone else. How dangerous it is to hold up the intimate knowledge of our imperfections against the outside packaging of others.

If there is one thing that living forty-plus years has taught me it's this: *All God's girls have issues. Every single one of us.*

But we can make the choice to identify our shortcomings and instead of using them against ourselves, hand them over to Jesus and let Him chisel our rough places.

The grace-filled way Jesus chisels is so vastly different from the way I mentally beat myself up.

My mental scripts are too often full of exaggerated lies that leave me feeling defeated. His chiseling is full of truth that sets me free.

Oh what a difference.

Jesus doesn't compare.

Jesus doesn't exaggerate.

Jesus doesn't condemn. Romans 8:1 confirms this: "There is now no condemnation for those who are in Christ Jesus." What grace.

He simply says, "Hey, I love you. I love you just how you are. But, I love you too much to leave you stuck in this. So let's work on it together. You can do this."

Having issues isn't the absence of victory in our lives. It's simply a call to action reminding us victory is right around the corner. Today is a great day to start believing you were made to walk in victory and to say to Jesus, "Yes, with Your truth as my guide, I can."

Dear Lord, help me see myself the way You see me. Remove the lies that defeat me more often than I want to acknowledge. You have set me free. Help me live like I truly believe that. In Jesus' Name, Amen.

47

If Only We Knew

We do not have a high priest who is unable to
empathize with our weaknesses, but we have one who
has been tempted in every way, just as we are—yet
he did not sin. Let us then approach God's throne of
grace with confidence, so that we may receive mercy
and find grace to help us in our time of need.

—HEBREWS 4:15–16

*H*ere is my prayer for you: *May you catch even the slightest glimpse of the tender mercy of our Lord Jesus. For one drop of the Lord's mercy is better than an ocean of the world's comfort.*

The situation that seems impossible.

The finances that never balance.

The hope so deferred it makes your heart sick.

The anxiety over a child bent on a wayward path.

The diet you are sick of.

The broken promises of a friend.

The lack of true friends.

The constant messiness always distracting from the peace you want in your home.

The impatience and frustration, anger and disappointment of losing it—again.

If only we knew how deeply Jesus understands and cares for us. If only we could see the wonder of His love. The skies He paints, the flowers He blooms, the world He arranges just for us. The love letters He's written to us throughout the Bible.

These are all mercies from Him.

The world will offer us comfort in the form of escapes. We escape to movies, magazines, malls, chocolate, vacations, affirmations from friends. Not that any of these things are bad. They aren't. But they are very temporary. They make us feel good in the moment, but that good never stays. We need more and more. Trying to fill our aching hearts with these things is like trying to fill an ocean with a tablespoon. It's never enough. So we clench our fists and keep trying to find something to comfort us.

If only we knew how to stop clenching our fists so that we could open our hands and catch the drops of His tender mercy. If only we knew how to release the weight of trying to fix it all ourselves. If only we knew to stop in the midst of it all and whisper, "Jesus . . . help me." Just a whispered breath formed in the wholeness of His Name carries all the power and mercy and wisdom and grace we need to handle what we face.

If only we knew.

If you find yourself wanting to escape today into one of the world's comforts, first invest some time in asking Jesus to help you, show you, and direct you. Hebrews 4:15–16 reminds us of how approachable He is, how He understands our struggles

> *One drop of the Lord's mercy is better than an ocean of the world's temporary comforts.*

and graciously offers us help and hope: "We do not have a high priest who is unable to empathize with our weaknesses, but we have one who has been tempted in every way, just as we are—yet he did not sin. Let us then approach God's throne of grace with confidence, so that we may receive mercy and find grace to help us in our time of need."

Specifically, ask Him to help you see and notice His tender mercies. Then you will see that, indeed, one drop of the Lord's mercy is better than an ocean of the world's temporary comforts.

Jesus, I don't want to spend another day chasing after things that will never satisfy. Instead, I pray that I would begin to truly see how high and how deep is the love You have for me. Help me catch the tender drops of Your mercy, and teach me how to fully embrace Your love. In Jesus' Name, Amen.

48

THE REAL PEACE WE NEED

On the evening of that first day of the week, when
the disciples were together, with the doors locked
for fear of the Jewish leaders, Jesus came and stood
among them and said, "Peace be with you!"

—JOHN 20:19

*W*hen Jesus rose from the grave and appeared in the midst of
His disciples meeting behind locked doors, I imagine they
were stunned, shocked, and overjoyed. With great intentionality, Jesus
chose the words He used to greet them. Of all the themes He could
have selected at that moment, He picked what they needed most.
What was it?

Joy?

Hope?

Love?

While all of these certainly would have been appropriate, Jesus
didn't touch on any of them. He simply said over and over again,
"Peace be with you!" According to John 20, it is the first thing He said.
He said it again before breathing on them to receive the Holy Spirit.
Then when addressing Thomas and his doubts, He said it yet again.

Each time Jesus is recorded as saying this, the writer ends the
sentence with an exclamation point. Not only was Jesus intentional,

He was also emphatic. His words were conveyed with great emphasis and urgency.

Why peace?

And why did Jesus use the particular phrase "Peace be with you!"?

I have a theory. This world is very good at conjuring up facades. Temporary moments of worldly happiness can appear joyful. The world takes hope and mistakes it for wishful thinking. And the world has made *love* an everyday word used to describe a feeling that can change quickly.

> The peace that flows despite circumstances can only be found through Jesus being with us.

The world's offering of joy, hope, and love is fleeting, temporary, and dangerously unstable, but it can put on a good show in the short term.

"I got that promotion—joy!"

"I think we can afford this house—hope!"

"He likes spending time with me—I think I'm in love!"

However, jobs can be lost in an instant, houses can be foreclosed on, and relationships can end.

So, really, what the world offers—for a moment or two—are false versions of joy, hope, and love.

But it cannot offer false peace. It can offer peaceful settings and rituals to conjure up peaceful thoughts, but not true soul contentedness. The peace that flows despite circumstances can only be found through Jesus being with us. That's why Jesus phrased it the way He did: "Peace be with you!" In other words, "You can walk through anything, My sweet daughter, if you realize that I am peace and I am with you."

Thank You, Lord, that You are peace and You are with me.
Help me remember that You are with me everywhere I go, no
matter what the day may bring. In Jesus' Name, Amen.

Part 3

Embracing Him in the Midst of Hurt & Heartbreak

49

I Have Trust Issues

God has said, "I will never fail you. I will never abandon
you." So we can say with confidence, "The Lord is my helper,
so I will have no fear. What can mere people do to me?"
—Hebrews 13:5–6 nlt

I want life to be as stable as a math problem. Two plus two always
equals four. It will equal four today, tomorrow, and into the tomorrows years from now.

Math equations don't experience heartbreaks and letdowns. They
don't get cancer. Or have their best friend get transferred and move
across the country. They are highly predictable. Therefore, they are
easy to trust.

But life doesn't add up. People don't add up. And in the rawest
moments of honest hurting, God doesn't add up. All of which makes
us hold our trust ever so close to our chests until it becomes more tied
to our fears than to our faith.

That's where I was when Bob and Maria stuck out their hands to
shake mine and invite me to their mountain home. I needed God to
untangle some of my trust issues.

They were having a retreat at their mountain home with an eclectic
group of some of their favorite people, and somehow I got on that list.

It was all going well until someone handed me a helmet. We were
about to do a ropes course.

And not just any old ropes course. The grand dismount of this course was a leap from a platform to catch a bar suspended several feet away. I started looking around for the emergency exit, because *there was no way on God's green earth they were going to get me to jump.*

And then Bob appeared. With his enormous smile, grandfather-gray hair, and arms magnetic with the purest grace, he drew me over to the edge.

"Lysa, this isn't about finishing the ropes course. This is about conquering your hesitancy, resistance, and fear. These ropes holding you will only let you slightly drop if you miss the bar. Then they will catch, and you absolutely will not fall," he whispered as if he had a window view inside of my soul.

What we see will violate what we know unless what we know dictates what we see.

I looked at the space between the edge of the platform and the bar. I saw death. Bob saw life.

What a visual for the word *trust.*

What we see will violate what we know unless what we know dictates what we see.

Bob knew the ropes would hold me. And he knew that my ability to survive this jump had absolutely nothing to do with my efforts. I was held safe standing on the platform. I would be held safe in midair. And I would absolutely be safe, whether or not I caught the bar.

Bob whispered, "You are absolutely loved. Now, when you're ready, jump."

I can't tell you how long I stood there. It felt like days and milliseconds all at the same time. The world swirled and tilted and shifted without me so much as twitching a muscle fiber. I forgot to breathe. I couldn't even blink.

I would imagine you've been in situations that have felt quite paralyzing as well. And it's in these times I have to tie my heart to soul-steadying verses like Hebrews 13:5–6: "God has said, 'I will never fail you. I will never abandon you.' So we can say with confidence, 'The LORD is my helper, so I will have no fear. What can mere people do to me?'" (NLT).

Just like those ropes wrapped around and around my body holding me to the course from beginning to end, God's Word can wrap our souls with steady assurance.

The peace of our souls does not have to rise and fall with unpredictable people or situations. Our feelings will shift, of course. People do affect us. But the peace of our souls is tethered to all that God is. And though we can't predict His specific plans, the fact that God will work everything together for good is a completely predictable promise.

Bob whispered one final thing: "It's already done."

I don't know exactly what he meant, but I know what my soul heard. *God has already caught me. His goodness and love have pursued me and won me. I just need to jump into that reality.* And without any other conscious thought, my soul kicked in where my brain could not. My feet exploded off the platform and into midair.

I touched the bar, but I did not catch it. I didn't need to. Because trust caught me.

Lord, I can't thank You enough for the promise that I can trust You at all times. Even though people may fail me, even though others may abandon me, You never will. I'm choosing to let that truth steady my heart today. In Jesus' Name, Amen.

50

IS GOD GOOD?

The Eternal is on His way:
    yes, He is coming to judge the earth.
He will set the world right by His standards,
    and by His faithfulness, *He will examine* the
    people.
        —PSALM 96:13 THE VOICE

I used to have a cautious approach to God. One look at the news, and one can quickly wonder, *How can a good God allow all this craziness, tragedy, and hurt?* For years, I would have answered, *What do I believe about God?* with a tilted head and a narrowed expression. "I believe He's unpredictable and slightly scary."

I didn't doubt God's power. I didn't doubt God's authority. But I did very much doubt God's goodness. However, when we go to the truth instead of our feelings for the answer to this question, we can understand God's goodness in a whole new light.

His goodness has been apparent since creation. When He formed and shaped and painted and sculpted this world and its creatures into being, His goodness seeped in with every thought and touch. "God saw all that he had made, and it was very good. And there was evening, and there was morning—the sixth day" (Genesis 1:31).

When Adam and Eve chose to sin, their sin infected and infiltrated the goodness of all God had made. So, while there are still good things in this world, the world is no longer a perfect reflection of God's goodness. In Romans 8:21 Paul explains that the world is in "bondage to decay" or, as some versions say, in "slavery to corruption" (NIV, THE VOICE). This decay and corruption are evidence of the brokenness of this world. I personally see this evidence every time swimsuit season cycles back around. Y'all, the cellulite is real! My body is in bondage to decay. But this is a conversation for another day.

God is good. His plans are good. His requirements are good. His salvation is good. His grace is good. His forgiveness is good. His restoration is good.

The world is in a state of decay and corruption. We see it in deadly weather patterns, natural disasters, and famines that were not part of God's good design. Cancer, sickness, and disease were not part of God's good design. Car accidents, drownings, and murders were not part of God's good design. The first sin did those things. When sin entered the world, it broke the goodness of God's design. And sin absolutely breaks God's heart. But in no way did sin affect the goodness of God. He has a plan, a good plan to rid this world of every effect of sin.

> The Eternal is on His way:
>   *yes*, He is coming to judge the earth.
> He will set the world right by His standards,
>   and by His faithfulness, *He will examine* the people. (Psalm 96:13 THE VOICE)

Though we may get our hearts broken from the effects of sin in this in-between time, God's goodness will eventually set the world right. In the meantime, we must hold fast to the truth of who God is and His unchanging nature: God is good. His plans are good. His requirements are good. His salvation is good. His grace is good. His forgiveness is good. His restoration is good. That is what I believe about God. God is good.

Dear Lord, You are good. Help me keep sight of Your goodness in the brokenness of this world. In Jesus' Name, Amen.

51

Is God Good to Me?

Those who live according to the flesh have their minds set
on what the flesh desires; but those who live in accordance
with the Spirit have their minds set on what the Spirit
desires. The mind governed by the flesh is death, but
the mind governed by the Spirit is life and peace.

—Romans 8:5–6

It's hard when you're a little girl desperate to be a treasured daughter but your dad makes it abundantly clear he never wanted a daughter.

I remember the prayers I would lift up when the darkness of night made my heart hammer in my chest. Tucked underneath my Holly Hobby blanket I would whisper over and over, "God, don't let my daddy leave me. Just don't let him leave me." Because if he did leave, who would I be? A girl without a daddy felt to me like a girl without a place in this world. After all, if he couldn't love me, who would ever love me?

I also remember the day my dad finally did stop coming home. The last bit of what held together my

I have to keep my mind focused on what the Holy Spirit whispers, not what my flesh screams.

security and my identity splintered as he packed his things without so much as looking at me. I pressed my face against the front window and watched his car fade into a blur. Then he was gone.

Rejection settled deep into my heart. And I came to one earth-shattering conclusion: *I don't matter. I am worth nothing to my dad.* And even more disturbing: *I fear I am worth nothing to God.* The sum of my feelings became my new identity.

Who is Lysa?

The unwanted one.

The years that followed only served to reinforce the hurt and questions residing in my heart. Based on my experiences with my dad not wanting me, I wondered what my heavenly Father's attitude was toward me. After all, how could God just stand by and allow so much heartbreak into one little girl's world? It seemed every three years starting the year my dad left, there was some kind of awful tragedy that cast lingering, dark shadows into my life. Abuse. Abandonment. Mental illness. The death of my sister. The cycle just kept going and going.

Even after I'd been a Christian for a long time and knew God loved me, I still had this nagging question about why the hard stuff had to be so painful. Was God really being good to me in this? I think C. S. Lewis said it best: "We are not necessarily doubting that God will do the best for us; we are wondering how painful the best will turn out to be."[1] And it's at this point someone at Bible study whips out Romans 8:28: "And we know that in all things God works for the good of those who love him, who have been called according to his purpose." I like that verse. And I think it helps shed some light on the reality that even if something doesn't feel good, God can still work good from it.

But verses 5 and 6 from this same chapter give me another layer of assurance: "Those who live according to the flesh have their minds set on what the flesh desires; but those who live in accordance with the Spirit have their minds set on what the Spirit desires. The mind governed by the flesh is death, but the mind governed by the Spirit is life and peace."

What doesn't feel good in my flesh won't make sense in my flesh. But if I have the Holy Spirit in me, my spirit is different because God is there—His indwelling presence with me. He speaks reassurances in the spirit. He speaks comfort in the spirit. He reminds me He is right there with me in the spirit. Others might disappoint me and leave me . . . but God never will. Therefore, I have to keep my mind focused on what the Holy Spirit whispers, not what my flesh screams. And in my spirit I know God is good to me.

Dear Lord, thank You for Your goodness to me.
When I am in pain, please help me remember Your
past faithfulness. In Jesus' Name, Amen.

52

DO I TRUST GOD TO BE GOD?

You will keep in perfect peace those whose minds are
steadfast, because they trust in you. Trust in the LORD
forever, for the LORD, the LORD himself, is the Rock eternal.
—ISAIAH 26:3–4

After my dad left, I tried to prop up what was left of me so I wouldn't collapse into the broken place inside. Good grades. Achievements and accolades. Fun friends and good times. Boys who made me feel special. I tried to steady myself with anything that helped me feel better.

But it wasn't just a better feeling that I needed; I needed a completely new way of defining my identity. I needed truth to inform what I believed about myself. Otherwise, what I believed about myself would become a fragile, flimsy, faulty foundation. The beliefs we hold should hold us up even when life feels like it's falling apart. So my old patterns of thought had to be torn out, and a new way of looking at the core of who I am using God's truth had to be put into place.

Our identity must be anchored to the truth of who God is and who He is to us. Only then can we find a stability beyond what our feelings will ever allow. The closer we align our truth with His truth, the more closely we identify with God—and the more our identity really is in Him.

In our previous two devotions we stabilized our identities by replacing old feelings with the solid truths that God is good and God is good to us. Now we have to answer one final question: do I trust God to be God?

This will not just stabilize our identities, but it will fully anchor us. I love these verses, Isaiah 26:3–4:

Our identity must be anchored to the truth of who God is and who He is to us.

> You will keep in perfect peace
>> those whose minds are steadfast,
>> because they trust in you.
> Trust in the LORD forever,
>> for the LORD, the LORD himself, is the Rock eternal.

The Hebrew word for *steadfast* used in verse 3 is *samak*, which means "to brace, uphold, support." Amazing, huh? In other words, those with minds fully braced, upheld, and supported by truth and trust in God will be kept in perfect peace.

Will I trust that God sees and knows things I don't? Will I trust Him when I don't understand? When circumstances are hard? When people betray or reject me? When my heart gets broken? Will I trust Him to the point where I fully turn the control of my life and those I love over to Him?

If God is good and God is good to me, then I must fill in the gaps of all the unknowns of my life with a resounding statement of trust: God is good at being God.

I don't have to figure my present circumstances out. I don't have to know all the whys and what-ifs. All I have to do is trust. So in quiet humility and without a personal agenda, I make the decision to let God sort it all out. I sit quietly in His presence and simply say, "God, I want Your truth to be the loudest voice in my life. Correct me. Comfort me. Come closer still. And I will trust. God, You are good at being God."

Dear Lord, I am so grateful that You are God and I am not! I trust in Your goodness. Thank You for the peace You give me. In Jesus' Name, Amen.

53

THE CRUSHING TIMES

We are hard pressed on every side, but not crushed;
perplexed, but not in despair; persecuted, but not
abandoned; struck down, but not destroyed.
—2 CORINTHIANS 4:8–9

*N*o one wants to have their heart crushed. But being wounded in deep places happens. Sometimes it just seems to be part of the rhythm of life.

And when these hard times come, we feel it all so very deeply. And we wonder if others have these hard, hard moments. After all, we don't snap pictures of the crushing times and post them on Instagram.

We just wonder if we have what it takes to survive . . .

. . . *when the doctor calls and says he needs to talk to me in person about the test results.*

. . . *when the teacher sends one of "those" emails about my child.*

. . . *when I feel so utterly incapable and unable and afraid.*

I suspect you know the tear-filled place from which I speak.

So, let's journey to the olive tree and learn.

To get to the place I want to take you, we must cross the Kidron Valley in Israel.

John 18:1–2 tells us, "When he had finished praying, Jesus left with his disciples and crossed the Kidron Valley. On the other side there was a garden, and he and his disciples went into it. Now Judas, who betrayed him, knew the place, because Jesus had often met there with his disciples."

Jesus often met in the shadow and shade of the olive tree in the garden.

This garden is the Garden of Gethsemane where Jesus, just before his arrest, said to Peter, James and John, "My soul is overwhelmed with sorrow to the point of death" (Mark 14:34).

Jesus knew the crushing-heart feeling. He felt it. He wrestled with it. He carried it.

And I don't think it was a coincidence that the olive tree was there in this moment of deep sorrow for Jesus.

The olive tree is such a picture of why our hearts must go through the crushing times.

The crushing times are necessary times.

First, in order to be fruitful the olive tree has to have both the east wind and the west wind. The east wind is the dry hot wind from the desert. This wind is so harsh that it can blow over green grass and make it completely wither in one day.

The west wind, on the other hand, comes from the Mediterranean. It brings rain and life.

The olive tree needs both of these winds to produce fruit—and so do we. We need both winds of hardship and relief to sweep across our lives if we are to be truly fruitful.

The crushing times are processing times.

Another thing to consider about the olive tree is how naturally bitter the olive is and what it must go through to be useful. If you were to pick an olive from the tree and try to eat it, its bitterness would make you sick.

For the olive to be edible, it has to go through a lengthy process that includes:

washing,
breaking,
soaking,
sometimes salting,
and waiting some more.

It is a lengthy process to be cured of bitterness and prepared for usefulness.

If we are to escape the natural bitterness of the human heart, we have to go through a long process as well . . . the process of being cured.

The crushing times are preservation times.

We need both the winds of hardship and relief to sweep across our lives if we are to be truly fruitful.

The best way to preserve the olive for the long run is to crush it in order to extract the oil. The same is true for us. The biblical way to be preserved is to be pressed. And being pressed can certainly feel like being crushed.

But what about 2 Corinthians 4:8, where it says we are "pressed . . . but not crushed"? Let's read verses 8 and 9 in the King James Version: "We are troubled on every side, yet not distressed; we are perplexed, but not in despair; persecuted, but not forsaken; cast down, but not destroyed."

This was one of the biggest "aha" moments for me standing in the shadow of the olive tree: crushing isn't the olive's end.

Crushing is the way of preservation for the olive. It's also the way to get what's most valuable, the oil, out of the olive. Keeping this perspective is how we can be troubled on every side yet not distressed . . . pressed to the point of being crushed but not crushed and destroyed.

I need to revisit these truths often:

When the sorrowful winds of the east blow, I forget they are necessary.

When I'm being processed, I forget it's for the sake of ridding me of bitterness.

And when I'm being crushed, I forget it's for the sake of my preservation.

I forget all these things so easily. I wrestle and cry and honestly want to resist every bit of this. Oh, how I forget.

Maybe God knew we all would forget.

And so, He created the olive tree.

Dear Lord, I'm so thankful that on the other side of the process of being broken and waiting is a useful heart free of bitterness. Help me to hold fast to You when the days are especially hard. In Jesus' Name, Amen.

54

WHAT I NEVER NOTICED ABOUT JESUS

Then he climbed into the boat with them, and the wind
died down. They were completely amazed, for they had not
understood about the loaves; their hearts were hardened.

—MARK 6:51–52

$\mathcal{I}$ ran my hand over the large rock and closed my eyes. What an incredible moment it was for me to stand where Jesus once stood in the Holy Land. I opened my Bible and let the full reality of all He was facing fall fresh on me.

I wanted to read the Scriptures leading up to this moment where He sat on Mount Arbel and prayed and watched the disciples, just before walking on water.

But I cautioned myself to read the uncommon sentences. Too many times I highlight verses telling of Jesus' miracles but skim right past those telling of deeply human realities.

In Mark chapter 5, we see Jesus interacting with a woman desperate to be healed from her bleeding disorder. He frees her from her suffering and gives her peace. And we find Him healing the young daughter of a synagogue ruler.

Miracle!

But we also find in verse 40, "But they laughed at him."

In Mark chapter 6 we see Jesus sending out the twelve disciples and as they preached, "They drove out many demons and anointed many sick people with oil and healed them" (v. 13).

Miracle!

But we also find earlier in verse 3, "And they took offense at him."

We find Him having great compassion on the people who followed Him in the feeding of the five thousand. They all ate and were satisfied by five loaves and two fish.

I get so focused on the mess, I miss the miracles.

Miracle!

But we also see that Jesus and His disciples were physically depleted, "because so many were coming and going that they did not even have a chance to eat" (v. 31).

Messy realities tucked in the midst of miracles.

And isn't it so like us to miss this about Jesus' everyday life? We hyper-focus on the lines of Scripture containing the miracles so much that we miss the detail of the mess.

Jesus had people laugh at Him and reject Him and misunderstand Him. We know this in theory, but as I sat on that rock that day I suddenly realized what an everyday reality this was for Him.

Now, here's what happens to me in my life: I get so focused on the mess, I miss the miracles.

And that's the very thing that happens to the disciples right after the feeding of the five thousand. They got in a boat and strong winds caused the water to get very rough. The disciples were straining at the oars as the realities of life beat against them.

Jesus was on the mountainside praying. From Mount Arbel, Jesus could see the middle of the lake where the disciples were. Mark

6:47–48 says, "Later that night, the boat was in the middle of the lake, and he was alone on land. He saw the disciples straining at the oars, because the wind was against them."

Jesus saw them. He went down to them. And they missed the miracle in the midst of the mess.

The same miracle worker that multiplied the fish and the loaves was now walking on the water near them and they thought He was a ghost. They were terrified and then were amazed, but they didn't understand, for the Scriptures say, "their hearts were hardened" (v. 52).

It seems to me Jesus has a pattern of performing miraculous acts in the setting of messes.

This revelation led me to a gut-honest prayer, *Oh Lord, let me see this. Please don't let the messes of life harden my heart and blind me to Your presence. Instead of being so terrified in the midst of the mess, might I keep the picture of You, watching me, always watching me. And might I find courage in the assurance that You will come to me with Your miraculous presence.*

Yes, I need to spend a whole lot less time trying to fix the messes in my life . . . and a whole lot more time keeping my heart soft in the process.

Then I won't miss the miraculous work of Jesus in the midst of my mess.

Dear Lord, You are so good. Help me see Your hand working even in the midst of things that seem to be messes. In Jesus' Name, Amen.

55

DEALING WITH DEEP GRIEF

The LORD is close to the brokenhearted
and saves those who are crushed in spirit.
—PSALM 34:18

osing someone you love can cut into your heart so viciously it forever redefines who you are and how you think. It's what I call *deep grief*.

It strains against everything you've ever believed. So much so, you wonder how the promises that seemed so real on those thin Bible pages yesterday could possibly stand up under the weight of this enormous sadness today.

I once stood at the side of a casket too small to accept. Pink roses draped everywhere. And I watched my mom as she lay across the casket refusing to let go. How could she let go? Part of her heart lay within, so quiet and so still.

I stood paralyzed and stunned. Just days ago we were laughing and doing everyday things and assuming that all of our lives stretched before us in spans of many, many years. And then suddenly . . . it all stopped.

In the flurry of funeral plans and memorial services we all operated on automatic. People were everywhere. Soft chatter filled in the gaps that our stunned silence could not. And people brought in enough food to feed the whole neighborhood.

But eventually people went back to their own lives. The soft chatter dissipated. The food stopped coming. And we were forced to carry on. Only we had deep grief wrapped about us that made our throats feel strangled and our feet stuck in mud.

Dear Lord, thank You for assuring me that Your promises hold true even when life seems to betray me.

I remember around that time when I tried to go to a drive-through to order some food. But I couldn't. I sat there with the speaker spouting words at me I couldn't process. The cashier kept asking if she could take my order.

Yeah, I had an order. Take away my bloodshot eyes. Take away my desire to hurt the doctors that couldn't save my little sister. Take away my anger toward God. And then take away my guilt for being the one who lived. *I'll take all that with no onions and extra ketchup, please.*

I drove away sobbing. *How dare they offer happy meals! No one should be happy today. Or tomorrow. Or next year.*

This is the reality of deep grief. Even when you love God and believe in His promises. Even when you know without a doubt that someday you will see your loved one again. Even when you know hope is still there. Even when you know He is near.

It takes time.

It takes wading through an ocean of tears.

It takes finding a possession of your loved one you thought was lost and realizing God did that just to comfort you. It takes discovering one day that the sun still shines. It takes being caught off guard when you catch yourself smiling, only to realize it's okay.

It takes prayer. It takes making the decision to stop asking for answers and start asking for perspective. It takes believing Psalm 34:18 is true even on the days it doesn't feel true—that the Lord is indeed close to the brokenhearted and saves those who are crushed in spirit. It takes telling people to please not avoid saying her name—you want to hear it, over and over and over again.

Then one day you take off the blanket of deep grief. You fold it neatly and tuck it away. You no longer hate it or resist it. For underneath it, wondrous things have happened over time. Things that could only have come about when Divine Hope intersects with a broken world.

And, finally, you can see years stretching before you once again. You look up, blow a kiss, wipe a tear, and find it's still possible to dance.

Dear Lord, thank You for assuring me that Your promises hold true even when life seems to betray me. You are my strength and my hope. In Jesus' Name, Amen.

56

WHY ISN'T GOD ANSWERING MY PRAYER?

*In the course of time Hannah became
pregnant and gave birth to a son.*
—1 SAMUEL 1:20

*H*ave you ever cried over something so much that you run out of tears? Your swollen eyes just give out and dry up while a current of unrest still gushes through your soul. And you look up toward heaven in utter frustration.

Me too.

And there's someone else in the Bible who was right there as well.

She felt provoked and irritated. Her anguish was so intense that she wept and would not eat. Before the Lord, she cried out in bitterness of soul, "LORD Almighty, if you will only look on your servant's misery and remember me, and not forget your servant . . . then I will . . ." (1 Samuel 1:11).

These words describe and articulate the deep distress of a woman from thousands of years ago, and yet here I sit in modern times relating so completely. They are from the woman named Hannah found in 1 Samuel 1.

Hannah's tears over her empty womb were made even more painful by her husband's other wife, Peninnah. She had many sons and daughters and made sure to rub this fact in Hannah's face every chance she got.

A common thread weaves through Hannah's story, and yours and mine. We can all be found desperately wanting something we see the Lord giving to other women. We see Him blessing them in the very areas He's withholding from us. We look at them and feel set aside.

God loves us too much to answer our prayers at any other time than the right time.

Why them? Why not me?

Then the seemingly unjust silence from God ushers us from a disturbed heart to a bitter soul. And we start to feel something deep inside that contradicts everything we hold true: *If God is good, why isn't He being good to me in this?*

And in this moment of raw soul honesty, we're forced to admit we feel a bit suspicious of God. We've done all we know to do. We've prayed all we know to pray. We've stood on countless promises with a brave face. And still nothing.

So what do we do when we feel set aside? What do we do when our hearts are struggling to make peace between God's ability to change hard things and His apparent decision not to change them for us?

We do what Hannah did. We keep pressing in.

Instead of taking matters into her own hands, Hannah took her requests to God. Instead of pulling away from Him in suspicion, she pressed in ever closer, filling the space of her wait with prayer.

Oh, how I love her unflinching faith. Where barrenness and mistreatment by Peninnah could have caused Hannah to completely lose heart, she refused to be deterred from trusting in God. She possessed a faith that was not contingent upon her circumstances, but based on what she knew to be true about her good and faithful God. A faith that led her to pray with so much passion and boldness in the tabernacle that Eli, the high priest, accused her of being drunk (1 Samuel 1:13–14)!

And in a matter of four verses (17–20), her cries of anguish gave way to the cries of her newborn son. Of course, 1 Samuel 1:20 uses very clear words to let us know Hannah's answer didn't come right away: "*In the course of time* Hannah became pregnant and gave birth to a son" (emphasis mine).

Samuel was born in God's perfect timing. And the timing of his birth was imperative because Samuel was destined to play an integral role in the transition from the time of the judges to the eventual establishment of kingship for the Israelites.

God hadn't made Hannah wait to punish her. He hadn't been callous or indifferent to her cries. And He's not ignoring those of us waiting either.

God loves us too much to answer our prayers at any other time than the right time.

Is there a prayer you've been waiting on God to answer for so long that you're just about ready to give up? Keep pressing in to Him, friend. Don't pull away. Fill the space where your heart aches with prayer, trusting that in the course of time everything will work out according to God's perfect plan.

Father God, thank You so much for reminding me today that You are not ignoring me. You hear every cry of my heart. Will You please help me in the waiting? Help me trust Your perfect timing. In Jesus' Name, Amen.

57

A Little Mad and a Lot Confused

From the ends of the earth I call to you,
I call as my heart grows faint;
lead me to the rock that is higher than I.
—Psalm 61:2

We talked in our last devotion about how hard it can be when God doesn't seem to be answering our prayers. Those times when our hearts hurt and our eyes leak while the "why" questions tumble in one after the other. And in those raw moments we can feel a little mad and a lot confused.

I don't want to oversimplify what to do in these times. I know from prayer requests I've received over the years many of us are facing tough issues. Situations where the answers aren't easy or clear-cut.

But I have discovered a few things that help me when God seems silent.

Press in to God when you want to pull away.

When I really want to hear from God but He seems silent, I sometimes find I want to disengage from my normal spiritual activities. Skip church. Put my Bible on my shelf. And let more and more time lapse between prayers.

Our God is big enough to handle our honest feelings.

But Psalm 61:2 reminds us that the best thing we can do when our hearts are growing faint is to call out to God, not pull away from Him. The Bible also promises we will find God if we seek Him with all our heart. Jeremiah 29:13, "You will seek me and find me when you seek me with all your heart." All my heart includes the parts that are broken. Bring it all to God.

He can handle your honesty and will respond. But we have to position ourselves to go where truth is. Go to church. Listen to praise music. Read verses. Memorize verses. And keep talking to God.

Praise God out loud when you want to get lost in complaints.

In the midst of what you're facing, find simple things for which to praise God. I don't mean thank Him for the hard stuff. I mean thank Him for the other simple, good things still in the midst. A child's laugh. A bush that blooms. The warmth of a blanket. The gift of this breath and then the next.

Psalm 40:3 reminds me God will give me a new song when I make praise the habit of my heart and mouth. "He put a new song in my mouth, a hymn of praise to our God. Many will see and fear the LORD and put their trust in him."

Put yourself in the company of truth.

That friend that speaks truth? Listen to her. Stay connected to her. Let her speak truth into your life even when you're tired of hearing it. Stand in the shadow of her faith when you feel your own faith is weak. Let her lead you back to God time and time again.

Proverbs 12:26, "One who is righteous is a guide to his neighbor" (ESV).

It's okay to feel a little mad and a lot confused. Our God is big enough to handle our honest feelings. But don't let your feelings lead you away from God or away from His truth. Press into Him. Praise Him. And put yourself in the company of truth.

As you stay with God in these ways, you will become ready to receive His answer when it comes.

Dear Lord, thank You for hearing every "why" my heart sends up to You. Forgive me when I retreat from You and Your Word. I want to trust You more. In Jesus' Name, Amen.

58

THE STING OF DISAPPOINTMENT

Though the fig tree does not bud
and there are no grapes on the vines,
though the olive crop fails
and the fields produce no food,
though there are no sheep in the pen
and no cattle in the stalls,
yet I will rejoice in the LORD,
I will be joyful in God my Savior.
—HABAKKUK 3:17–19

Recently a friend asked me if I ever get disappointed. I said yes and threw out a spiritually sound answer. Then the next day it happened. A huge disappointment whacked me upside the head and sent my heart sinking. I'd been asked to be part of a really big event—one of the biggest of my life—and then things fell apart.

Invited, thrilled, excited, honored, and included, turned into . . . uninvited, bummed, saddened, disillusioned, and left out. And while I still had solid spiritual perspectives to hold on to, my flesh just needed a minute to say, "Stink!"

Because sometimes things do stink. And disappointments come up that make us doubt God really does work for our good.

Right when I wanted to say "stink" a few more times, I spotted

I'd rather rejoice in what is and what will be, than wallow in what isn't.

a bowl that'd been sitting on my dining room table for a while. My daughter Brooke found some caterpillars weeks before, put them in a bowl, and had been holding them hostage ever since. I mean, she'd been lovingly admiring them underneath a layer of cellophane.

Wouldn't you know that those caterpillars formed cocoons inside that unlikely environment. And then, as I was muttering, "Stink!" I glanced across the table to that bowl and sucked the word back down my throat.

The cocoons were empty.

Expecting glorious butterflies, I was confused when I got right over the bowl and closely examined the product of my little girl's hopes for new life.

Moths.

I just had to chuckle. Yet another thing in my day that wasn't quite right.

Or was it?

When Brooke spotted the moths, she was beyond thrilled. Grabbing my hand, she led me outside, ripped off the plastic barrier, and watched the beauty of tiny wings beating . . . beating . . . beating . . . and finally fluttering into flight.

Hmmmm.

As I watched Brooke's sheer delight, I realized she couldn't have cared less if they were moths or butterflies. Creatures that once only knew the dirt of the earth had just been given the gift of flight. Reaching, soaring up, up, and away.

And with that realization, this simple creature pulled up the corners of her mouth into a smile.

Her reaction challenged me to look at my situation with fresh eyes, much like our key verse does:

> Though the fig tree does not bud and there are no grapes on the vines, though the olive crop fails and the fields produce no food, though there are no sheep in the pen and no cattle in the stalls, yet I will rejoice in the LORD, I will be joyful in God my Savior. (Habakkuk 3:17–19)

In the midst of all that's disappointing or heartbreaking in our lives, we can fix our eyes on all that seems to be going wrong or we can choose to purposefully praise God with a heart of trust. A heart that remembers He is loving, He is good, and He sees much more purpose in our situation than we do.

I decided to take one step away from disappointment and take one step toward the good God was working through the loss of the speaking event. I don't know why that amazing opportunity was offered to me, only to be taken away. But I do know this: I'd rather rejoice in what is and what will be, than wallow in what isn't. After all, disappointment only stings as long as I let it.

Dear Lord, thank You for Your mercies and patience in this journey of imperfect progress. Forgive me for allowing disappointment to capture my heart so easily. Adjust my perspective and help me to see the things You have brought to life in me. In Jesus' Name, Amen.

59

WHY WOULD GOD LET THIS HAPPEN?

"Though the mountains be shaken
and the hills be removed,
yet my unfailing love for you will not be shaken
nor my covenant of peace be removed,"
says the LORD, who has compassion on you.

—ISAIAH 54:10

I wonder what would happen in our lives if we really lived in the absolute assurance of God's love. I mean, as Christians we know He loves us. We sing the songs, we quote the verses, we wear the T-shirts and we sport the bumper stickers. Yes, God loves us.

I'm not talking about knowing He loves us.

I'm talking about living as if we really believe it.

I'm talking about walking confidently in the certainty of God's love even when our feelings beg us not to.

I'm talking about training our hearts and our minds to process everything through the filter of the absolute assurance of God's love. Period. Without the possible question mark.

Not too long ago, I had a conversation with a precious mom whose eldest daughter is nearing thirty and has never had a boyfriend. The younger siblings have all gone through the whole dating thing and one is now engaged to be married. The eldest daughter sat on the side of her mom's bed recently with tears slipping down her cheeks and said, "Why mom? Why can't I find anyone to love me? What's wrong with me?"

This mom was asking me for advice in helping her daughter process these questions. These feelings are real. These feelings are tough.

And I'm sure if I were able to untangle all the emotions wrapped in and around these questions, somewhere deep inside I would find this girl doubting God's love for her.

But here's the thing I've learned through my own heartbreak and doubt . . . we must process our hurts

We must process our hurts through the filter of God's love, not through the tangled places of our hearts.

through the filter of God's love, not through the tangled places of our hearts.

When we process things through the tangled places of our hearts, often the outcome is, *If God loves me so much, why would He let this happen?* Instead when we process things through the filter of the absolute assurance of God's love, the outcome is, *God loves me so much, therefore I have to trust why He is allowing this to happen.*

I took the mom's hand who was asking for advice and told her to help her daughter rewrite the way she is processing this. It's okay to feel hurt, lonely, and sad. But these feelings shouldn't be a trigger to doubt God's love for her. They should be a trigger to look for God's protection, provision, and possible growth opportunities.

I know this can be hard. But what if we really lived in the absolute assurance of God's love? Oh, sweet sister, in whatever you are facing today I pray Isaiah 54:10 over you, "Though the mountains be shaken and the hills be removed, yet God's unfailing love for you will not be shaken."

> *Dear Lord, You are good. And You are good at being God. Therefore, I trust Your plan and believe that You're allowing this to happen for a reason. It may be hard, but I'd rather be close to You through a thousand difficult moments than apart from You in a thousand good ones. In Jesus' Name, Amen.*

60

What Makes Rejection So Awful?

"I have come into the world as a light, so that no one
who believes in me should stay in darkness."
—John 12:46

*M*y mouth was dry. My hands a bit numb. There was a stabbing
tightness in my chest. My mind blurred as my thoughts became
a fragmented kaleidoscope of a million pictured hopes I thought were
just around the corner for me. For us. For the us that was now becoming . . . just me again.

We were only dating. But my mind had already run ahead in time
and built a life with this man. In the future we had romantic picnics
to take, snowball fights to laugh through, a wedding to plan, a house
to build, and kids to name with his smile and my eyes.

I'm not sure these were ever real to him. But to me, they were as
real as the stone-cold coffee now sitting in front of me. The one I kept
stirring to have something to focus on but that I never intended to
drink. Drinking coffee seemed a bit too normal when my entire inner
life had just been declared a state of emergency. Because suddenly,
the rest of my planned-out life was aflame. I wasn't just losing a boyfriend today. I was losing the connection to my dreams for tomorrow
that would never be.

His words made their way through my ears to my heart. I felt

*Just because
I've been hurt
doesn't mean
I now have
to live hurt.*

the full impact of their harsh landing. As they skidded their way across the most tender places inside me, their piercing weight burned and cut and ripped apart what I thought would be so very permanent. Rejection always leaves the deepest, darkest marks.

That was decades ago. But I can pull up that memory as if it were yesterday. I have to search a bit in my past, but there it is. The wound is no longer pulsing with pain. It's more of a scar. Like a war wound, it's just a story now.

I pulled out my journal today and tried to capture the raw essence of what makes rejection so awful. But I couldn't capture the depth of it with finely crafted words. Instead of diving deep with my thoughts, I let them come in simple, personal phrases:

I like stability.
I don't like getting caught off guard.
I like feeling known.
I don't like feeling thrown away.

As I wrote this list, one line finally emerged to sum up rejection better than the others: *I don't want my normal to be snatched away.* Life feels impossibly risky when I'm reminded how unpredictable circumstances can shatter and forever change what I know and love about my life. And in the fallout, some pieces never fall back into place.

It's like taking a photograph containing all the people you love and suddenly, some of them purposely cut themselves out of the picture. The gaping hole left behind in some ways is worse than death. If they'd passed away, you would grieve their loss. But when their absence is caused by rejection, you not only grieve their loss but also wrestle through the fact that they wanted this. *They chose to cut themselves out.*

Though you're devastated, they're walking away feeling relieved. Or worse, they might even feel happy. And there you sit, staring at a jacked-up photograph no glue in the world can fix. Normal? Taken. Not by accident. But very much on purpose from someone you never expected could be such a thief.

Rejection steals the security of all we thought was beautiful and stable and leaves us scared, fragile, and more vulnerable than ever.

But God. He's there. Jesus said, "I have come into the world as light, so that no one who believes in me should stay in darkness" (John 12:46). With Jesus I can walk out of this dark place.

Yes, He is the One who can help me. Heal me. Show me what to do when I'm hurting. Therefore, I must do whatever He instructs me to do. I must embrace Him. And I know I can't continue to fully embrace God while rejecting His ways.

So I turn to Him. And really listen to where He's leading with a willing heart.

God drops a word into my heart. Like a swig of orange juice just after brushing my teeth, I recoil at the unexpected taste. Of grace.

Why grace?! Because grace given when it feels least deserved is the only antidote for bitterness. Just because I've been hurt doesn't mean I now have to live hurt. I can get mad and bitter and spread more hurt around. Or, I can choose grace and gentle responses and spread more hope around.

Hurt people, hurt people.

Healed people, heal people.

And I want to be in that latter group.

There's nothing we can do to eliminate the pain of rejection. Oh, how I wish there were. With every fiber of my being, I wish I could remove it from my world and yours. But I can't. The only thing to help my heart heal from these deep wounds is the constant pursuit of the sweetest grace.

To love God is to cooperate with His grace. And since I'm so very aware of my own need for grace, I must be willing to freely give it away. Each hole left from rejection is an opportunity to create more and more space for grace in my heart.

Father God, please help me be a woman who is quick to give grace, even when it's the last thing I want to do. Thank You for the grace You extend to me each and every day. In Jesus' Name, Amen.

61

IF YOU EVER FEEL LONELY, READ THIS

Turn to me and be gracious to me,
for I am lonely and afflicted.
The troubles of my heart are enlarged;
bring me out of my distresses.
—PSALM 25:16–17 ESV

*T*here were many feelings I expected to have at a conference I'd been looking forward to attending. Acceptance. Fun. Camaraderie.

On paper, these were my people.

They lead organizations. I lead an organization. They are vulnerable. I am vulnerable. Like me, they know the stresses of deadlines, trying to balance kids with ministry, and the nagging sense that we should keep hidden the fact that we have the pizza delivery place on speed dial.

Yes. I couldn't wait to be with these people.

And I couldn't wait for the deep friendships that would surely bloom as a result of our time together.

I walked into the meeting room and quickly located the table of the people I was excited to meet. Every seat had a nametag attached so I circled the table looking for mine. As I got to the last chair and realized my name wasn't there, I got a sinking feeling.

I milled around the room looking for my name, feeling increasingly out of place. Finally, at a table on the opposite side of the room, I found my name. I rallied in my heart that the Lord must have a special plan for me to meet and connect with the others assigned to my table. I took my seat and pulled out my cell phone as I nervously waited for my tablemates.

I waited.

And waited.

And waited.

As the prayer for the meal concluded and the event got underway it became painfully apparent to me that the others assigned to my table weren't able to come for some reason. So, I'd be seated alone. *Very* alone.

> *There is something wonderfully sacred that happens when a girl chooses to look past being set aside to see God's call for her to be set apart.*

In reality, I don't think anyone else really noticed my predicament. After all, by this time everyone in the room was busy passing rolls and salad dressings.

In my head I started to have a little pity conversation: *Well, self, would you like a roll? Or ten perhaps? It's certainly an option when you're sitting single at a table for ten.*

And that's when a very clear sentence popped into my head: *You aren't set aside, Lysa. You are set apart.* It wasn't audible. And it wasn't my own thought. I knew it was a thought assigned by God that I needed to ponder.

To be set aside is to be rejected.

That's exactly what the Enemy would have wanted me to feel. If he could get me to feel this, then I'd become completely self-absorbed in my own insecurity and miss whatever reason God had for me to be at this event.

To be set apart is to be given an assignment that requires preparation.

That's what I believe God wanted me to see. If He could get me to see this, I'd be able to embrace the lesson of this situation.

Have you ever been in this place?

I wasn't just in this place at the dinner that night. I've been in whole seasons of my life where, though I had people around, I felt quite alone in my calling.

Can I give you three thoughts that might encourage you today?

1. Look for the gift of being humbled. Proverbs 11:2 reminds us that "with humility comes wisdom." In this set-apart place, God will give you much-needed special wisdom for the assignment ahead.

2. Look for the gift of being lonely. This will help you develop a deeper sense of compassion for your fellow travelers. You better believe when I walk into a conference now, I look for someone sitting alone and make sure they know someone noticed them.

3. Look for the gift of silence. Had I been surrounded by the voices of those people I was so eager to meet that night, I would have surely missed the voice of God. I'm trying to weave more silence into the rhythm of my life now so I can whisper, "God, what might You want to say to me right now? I'm listening."

I know it can be painful to be alone. And I know the thoughts of being set aside are loud and overwhelmingly tempting to believe in the hollows of feeling unnoticed and uninvited.

But as you pray through your feelings, ask God exactly what the psalmist does in Psalm 25:16–17—*to turn to you and be gracious to you* in your loneliness. And then see if maybe your situation has more to do with you being prepared than overlooked.

There is something wonderfully sacred that happens when a girl chooses to look past being set aside to see God's call for her to be set apart.

Dear Lord, help me see the gifts hidden in this season of loneliness. I'm believing today that I'm set apart, not set aside. In Jesus' Name, Amen.

62

THE GIRL CALLED LOSER

Holy brothers and sisters, who share in the heavenly
calling, fix your thoughts on Jesus, whom we
acknowledge as our apostle and high priest.
—HEBREWS 3:1

The year was 1982. I was in the seventh grade.

With frizzy brown hair and buckteeth, I walked down the pea-green hallway of my middle school. It was the day after student council elections.

The day *after* my classmates confirmed what I'd so desperately feared: If you didn't have beauty and a boyfriend, no one would vote for you.

I shuffled toward my locker, wishing I were invisible. I kept my eyes down while I willed my feet to just keep walking. Finally, my locker was in sight. That glorious metal box was where I could sort of escape this world of critical girls with cute outfits and spiral-permed hair. I could hide my face, let the tears slip, and pretend to be busy shuffling books.

But instead of finding respite in that tiny metal space, I found one of my election posters plastered to the front, with the word "loser" scrawled

No amount of outward success can give you inward acceptance.

across the top. *How do you quickly hide a poster-sized proclamation by the world that you aren't good enough, cool enough, pretty enough, or accepted enough?*

Books dropping, girls laughing, tape ripping, and poster crunching were the sounds throbbing in my ears as the poster board resisted my attempts to ball it up small enough to fit into the mouth of the hallway trash can.

Please fit, please fit, please fit! Oh God, please help this stupid poster from this stupid election with my stupid face on it disappear into this stupid trash can!

The bell rang. And as all the "normal" people scampered past me, I heard Stephanie's voice like a dagger's deathblow whisper, "Loser."

I turned and saw my one confidant. My one friend. My one secret-holder, being welcomed into the popular girls' circle. Her public rejection of me was her ticket in to the crowd we'd secretly loathed together. *Together.*

I sank beside the trash can where the poster slowly untwisted on the ground in front of me. *Loser.*

I remembered this one night recently as I sat in front of a group of young high school students. Girls who vulnerably shared how hard peer relationships can be. They described tangled relationships and feelings of loneliness so consuming they sometimes wished the world would open up and swallow them whole.

I understood their feelings all too well. I have known the sting of loneliness. I knew it in middle school and I know it now in adulthood. Relationships can be hard no matter what your age.

And here's the real kicker.

I always thought my ticket to acceptance would have come had I won that school election. Not so. For I've discovered on the other side of achievements, if you were lonely before you win, you'll be lonely after you win. No amount of outward success can give you inward acceptance.

I've only been able to find that in the comfort of Jesus.

One quick glance at our key verse confirms that Jesus is exactly the One we need to look to—"Holy brothers and sisters, who share in the heavenly calling, fix your thoughts on Jesus, whom we acknowledge as our apostle and high priest" (Hebrews 3:1).

Thoughts fixed on, heart filled with, life defined by Jesus.

Jesus.

The One who will never reject us. The One who knows what it feels like to be rejected—though He should have been the most accepted. The One who will sit with us and remind us rejection from man doesn't equal rejection from God. The One who whispers to each of us, "The voices of shame and rejection can come at you, but they don't have to reside in you."

I wish I could go back and preach this truth to my seventh-grade self, but since I can't, I'll preach it to my grown-up heart. And to yours too. We are *loved.* And no person's rejection can ever take that love away from us.

Father God, thank You for the reminder that I don't have to let the labels from others stick to me. You say I am loved. You say I am chosen. You say I'm forever Yours. And Yours is the voice I'm choosing to believe. In Jesus' Name, Amen.

63

YESTERDAY'S HURTS IN
TODAY'S RELATIONSHIPS

*My dear brothers and sisters, take note of
this: Everyone should be quick to listen, slow
to speak and slow to become angry.*
—JAMES 1:19

"W*e don't need you there."*

A simple sentence. Five words. Five syllables. However, in my brain the interpretation of this sentence was anything but simple.

It unleashed a flood of uncertainty. My brain instantly fired off locator arrows that traveled to past rejections in my memory. Pulling past hurts into the current conversation. Suddenly, I wasn't hearing *"We don't need you there."* I was hearing, *"You aren't wanted."*

Rejection always wants to steal the best of who I am by reinforcing the worst of what's been said to me.

The best of who I am was certainly not the one interpreting this comment.

The most hurt version of me took what was said and added pages of commentary. This additional dialogue highlighted my insecurities, brought to mind all the many reasons I was surely being excluded, and vilified the person who uttered those five words that started this whole thing.

Suddenly, this person was unsafe. She was insensitive. And worst of all, I pictured her rallying others to believe the worst about me as well.

I blinked back my tears. I swallowed the long-winded speech I was dying to spew in retaliation to her hurtful proclamation. And with a simple, "Okay," I walked to my car.

Later that night I retold the whole story to a member of my family. With great emotion and lots of added commentary, I gave them the play-by-play. Finally, I paused long enough to catch my breath and fully expected them to jump right in with absolute support and an offer to rush to my defense.

Instead they said, "What else might she have meant by her statement? Is there any chance she didn't intend to hurt you, but rather was just simply stating the fact that they had enough people participating and you didn't have to feel the pressure to attend?"

I shot back, "Oh no, I'm telling you this was *so much more* than that."

Right as I was about to unleash another dramatic retelling of the whole situation, they stopped me and said, "Just make sure you aren't holding her accountable for words she never said. She didn't say you weren't wanted. She didn't say you weren't capable. She didn't say others were thinking the same way as her. She simply said they didn't need you there."

After stewing for a while, I dared to consider what my family member had said. I called the gal and asked a few questions. And in the end, I realized there was absolutely no agenda behind her statement at all.

In fact, she thought she was doing me a favor by assuring me that I wasn't

Rejection always wants to steal the best of who I am by reinforcing the worst of what's been said to me.

needed so that I wouldn't feel pressure to be gone from home during that very busy season.

This situation happened eight years ago, but I think about it often. It taught me three perspectives that I don't want to forget:

1. When I'm tired or stressed, I'm likely to interpret interactions way more emotionally than I should. Therefore, I should wait to respond to others until I've had a chance to rest and de-stress. A depleted girl can quickly become a defeated girl when she lets emotions dictate her reactions.

That's one of the reasons I love today's key verse and the way it interrupts me: "My dear brothers and sisters, take note of this: Everyone should be quick to listen, slow to speak and slow to become angry" (James 1:19).

2. Believe the best before assuming the worst. Even if they didn't have my best interest in mind, they probably didn't have the worst intentions either. Regardless, being positive will keep me in a much better place.

3. Clarify. Clarify. Clarify. When in doubt, I should ask them to help me understand what they truly meant. And when I clarify, I must recognize and resist adding any additional commentary my past hurt might add to this situation.

Can you think of a time in your life when these perspectives might help? I certainly haven't perfected making these perspectives the first thing I think of when I'm in an uncertain situation. But at least I do think of them. And that's great progress, so feelings from yesterday's hurts don't take away from today's relationships.

Dear Lord, I don't want to allow hurts from my past or runaway emotions to steal from my present relationships. I surrender my heart to You today— asking for Your wisdom and healing touch. In Jesus' Name, Amen.

64

There's a Lady at the Gym Who Hates Me

The LORD your God is in your midst,
a mighty one who will save;
he will rejoice over you with gladness;
he will quiet you by his love;
he will exult over you with loud singing.

—ZEPHANIAH 3:17 ESV

There's a lady at my gym who hates me.

No, I'm serious. She sees me coming, and I can feel little poofs of disdain chugging out of her ears as her feet churn at eighty-seven miles per hour on the elliptical machine. I honestly don't know how she goes so fast. I once tried to keep up with her.

It was awful.

And I think that was the day her infuriation with me began.

Let me back up and confess my sins that started this whole thing.

The elliptical machines are very close together and completely awkward with their angular moving parts. Think if a New York high-rise and an elephant had a baby; that would be these elliptical machines.

Now, conjure up a picture in your mind of the most athletic person you know. The one who doesn't have a drop of fat on her entire body, not even at her belly button, which should be illegal in my cellulite-ridden opinion. Okay, do you have your person?

That's her. She's honestly stunningly beautiful.

Then picture a marshmallow dressed in a T-shirt and spandex pants. Her ponytail is rather tight, but not much else is. That's me. Hello, world.

So, I had to sort of get in her space just a tad to mount my machine, and I think I threw off her rhythm. That was sin number one.

Then I decided to try to stay in sync with her because I wanted to teach all the folks at the gym that, though my legs and derrière might not look like it, I'm in shape. That was sin number two.

And then there may have been a little issue with me taking a phone call while working out. In my defense, this is not at all my common practice. But a friend called who really needed me.

Live from the abundant place where you are loved, and you won't find yourself begging others for scraps of love.

I tried to chat quietly, but when you feel like a lung might very well pop out of your mouth at any minute, it's difficult to whisper-talk. Sin number three.

Three strikes, and she deemed me out. Out of my mind. Out of line. Out of control.

She abandoned her elliptical and huffed over to the treadmill.

And I think she's hated me ever since. But then the other day, something occurred. Something odd that stunned me.

She smiled at me.

It wasn't an evil, I'm-about-to-whip-your-tail-on-the-gym-floor kind of smile. It was more like an, "Oh hey, I've seen you here before, right?" kind of smile.

And the more I've thought about it, the more I've realized her hating me has all been a perception thing on my part.

Which got me thinking about all the many times I assign thoughts to others that they never actually think. I hold them accountable to harsh judgments they never make. And I own a rejection from them they never gave me.

I know not every rejection is like this. Some are completely certified and undeniable.

But we have to know there are also perceived rejections, like I had with my fellow gym-goer.

I don't even think I was really on her radar.

But in my mind, I was absolutely in her crosshairs. And so goes the crazy inside our heads sometimes.

Thankfully, the Lord reminds us in our key verse that He is able to "quiet" our crazy thoughts with His love.

It makes me remember something I saw an author friend of mine do several years ago when she was signing a book. Her approach was simple. Before signing her name she wrote, "Live loved."

Not only an instruction, but a proclamation. One that arrests my soul and is so applicable to our discussion at hand.

Live from the abundant place where you are loved, and you won't find yourself begging others for scraps of love.

It's not deciding in your mind, *I deserve to be loved.* Or manipulating your heart to feel loved.

It's settling in your soul, *I was created by a God who formed me because*

He so very much loved the very thought of me. When I was nothing, He saw something and declared it good. Very good. And very loved.

This should be the genesis thought of every new day.

I am loved.

Not because of how terrific I am. God doesn't base His affection on my wilted efforts.

No, God's love isn't based on me.

It's simply placed on me.

And it's the place from which I should live . . . loved.

Dear Lord, I'm so grateful I don't have to walk around all day trying to figure out who likes me and who doesn't. I can simply rest in the truth that I am completely and perfectly loved by You. Help me to live loved today. In Jesus' Name, Amen.

65

BECAUSE I AM LOVED

Do nothing out of selfish ambition or vain conceit. Rather, in
humility value others above yourselves, not looking to your
own interests but each of you to the interests of the others.

—PHILIPPIANS 2:3–4

A few years ago, my friend challenged me with this question: Are
you doing this *because* you *are* loved or *so that* you'll be loved?
Her question is a great one.

Doing something "so that we'll be loved" is a trap many of us can
get caught in. When I do something because I'm trying to get someone else to notice me, appreciate me, say something to build me up or
respect me more, my motives get skewed.

I forget the reminder in Philippians 2:3–4 to do nothing out of
selfish ambition and to look to the interests of others. Instead, I
become very "me" focused. I put unrealistic expectations on myself
and the other person. And I can get so very hurt when I don't feel more
noticed, appreciated, or respected.

But, doing something because I
am loved is incredibly freeing.

I don't view the relationship from
the vantage point of what I stand to
gain. Instead, I look at what I have

> *Are you doing this
> because you are
> loved or so that
> you'll be loved?*

the opportunity to give. I am "God-focused" and love-directed. I keep my expectations in check. And I am able to lavish the grace I know I so desperately need. I live free from regret with clarity of heart, mind, and soul.

So, how do I know if I'm doing things because I'm loved or so that I will be loved? See how easy or hard it is to apply these biblical truths:

Because I am loved, I can humble myself. When I'm trying to be loved, I must build myself up to look better.

Because I am loved, I can cast all my anxiety on Him. When I'm trying to be loved, I cast all my anxiety on my performance.

Because I am loved, I can resist Satan and stand firm in my faith. When I'm trying to be loved, I listen to Satan and stand uncertain trying to rely on my feelings.

Because I am loved, I know God will use this to make me stronger—and I want that. When I'm trying to be loved, I don't want to be made stronger—I want life to be easier.

Yes, I want to pursue life, relationships, and the goals I set from a healthy and free vantage point—because I am loved.

These aren't just good life principles, they're God's life principles.

Dear Lord, I don't want my motives to get skewed today. Help me not be so "me-focused." I want to live each day knowing I am loved. Living because I am loved is freeing. I long to stop trying so hard. I know You love me, Lord, and that You are making me stronger. Thank You. In Jesus' Name, Amen.

Alone in a Crowded Room

"A new command I give you: Love one another. As I have loved you, so you must love one another."
—John 13:34

I wished the small room would open up and swallow me whole. Just envelop me into an abyss that would simultaneously hide me and remove me.

It's painful to be in a crowded room and feel all alone.

Everyone had someone. Their chatting and laughing lilted in a symphony of connection. I looked around, and there wasn't a soul I recognized.

My brain demanded I just walk up and introduce myself to someone—anyone. But my heart sensed they were all knee-deep in conversations that would be super awkward for me to break into.

Isn't it strange how you can literally rub shoulders with lots of people but feel utterly alone? Proximity and activity don't always equal connectivity.

On the surface, connectivity seems to require that I connect with other people, and they connect back with me. Of course that gathering was an extreme example of being alone in a crowded room, but that feeling isn't sequestered to that one incident.

I can get it when things grow cold and too quiet with a family

Proximity and activity don't always equal connectivity.

member. And deep down inside of me, I want to ask for forgiveness, but my pride is holding all my kind words hostage. So the silent treatment continues. And though we're in the same house, we're nowhere near connecting.

Or that feeling can happen when I'm with a group of women, and I can't quite seem to break into the conversation. I mentally beat myself up for not being more brilliant, or caught up on the world's current events and fashion trends. They all seem so effortlessly on top of everything.

In each of these situations I'm with people. But I'm so very alone.

And I secretly ponder how the events of that day clearly point out other people's issues: their self-focus, their past problems, their insensitivity.

But the problem wasn't the people at the party. The problem wasn't my family or that group of women. It was me not being prepared in advance with a fullness that can only come from God.

It was as if I walked into each of these situations suddenly feeling like I wouldn't be able to breathe unless someone else invited me in. The whole room was full of completely breathable air, but since I refused to take it in, I suffered.

I can't expect any other person to be my soul oxygen. I can't live as if my next breath depends on whether or not they give me enough air for my lungs not to be screaming in pain.

No, it's not wrong to need people. But some of our biggest disappointments in life are the result of expectations we have for others, which they can't ever possibly meet. That's when the desire to connect becomes an unrealistic need.

Here's the secret shift I've learned we must make:

Do I walk into situations prepared with the fullness of God in me, free to look for ways to bless others?

Or . . .

Do I walk into situations empty and dependent on others to look for ways to bless me?

People prepared with the fullness of God in them are not super-people with pixie-dust sparkles of confidence. No, the fullness of God is tucked into the sacred places within them. The full taking in of God is their soul oxygen. It's not that they don't need people. They do. God created them for community. But the way they love is from a full place, not from an empty desperation. They live loved.

And this is how I want to live too.

Being full of God's love settles, empowers, and brings out the best of who we are.

Like I said before, when we live from the abundant place where we are loved, we won't find ourselves begging others for scraps of love. We'll be ready and able to walk into a room and live out Jesus' command in John 13:34 to love one another—sharing the love we already know is ours.

Dear Lord, thank You so much for the way You love me—with a love that can never be shaken, taken, or tarnished. Help me look to You and You alone to fill and satisfy my heart. In Jesus' Name, Amen.

67

THREE THINGS YOU MUST REMEMBER WHEN REJECTED

The righteous person may have many troubles,
but the LORD delivers him from them all.
—PSALM 34:19

I scooted into the restaurant booth beside my daughter Ashley. Her first-semester college grades had been posted for two days, but she'd refused to look at them. We decided to review them together at one of our favorite restaurants.

Together is a great way to press through something you're afraid could make you feel a bit undone.

School hasn't always been easy for Ashley. When she was in the eighth grade, her teachers requested a meeting. I was stunned to find out she was failing every class.

It wasn't from her lack of effort. She simply wasn't grasping the new curriculum her school had switched to that year. And their only suggestion was to have her go back and repeat seventh grade.

Immediately, I knew that would never work. I also think the school knew this wouldn't work. So they offered to help us have her transferred to a different school.

It wasn't intended as a rejection. But it sure felt like one.

Yet slowly, little successes at her new school gave her enough confidence to believe it was possible to turn things around. And by the end of that year, she was on the dean's list. By the time she got into high school, she was making great grades and even graduated with honors.

Satan knows what consumes us controls us.

Now in college, she'd chosen an academically rigorous major. She'd given it her all. But the exams all carried a lot of weight toward her overall grades, and she just wasn't sure how she'd done. And though that eighth-grade rejection was very far from her at that point, the fear still lingered.

The Enemy loves to take our rejection and twist it into a raw, irrational fear that God really doesn't have a good plan for us.

This fear is a corrupting companion. It replaces the truths we've trusted with hopeless lies. Satan knows what consumes us controls us. Therefore, the more consumed we are with rejection, the more he can control our emotions, our thinking, and our actions.

So what's a brokenhearted person to do? We must take back control from something or someone that was never meant to have it and declare God as Lord. To help us see how we can practice this when the worries of rejection try to control us, here are three things to remember and proclaim.

1. One rejection is not a projection of future failures. It's good to acknowledge the hurt, but don't see it as a permanent hindrance. Move on from the source of the rejection, and don't let it shut you down in that arena of life. It has already stolen enough from your present. Don't let it reach into your future.

Replace the negative talk that will hinder you. Replace it with praises for God, who will deliver you.

2. There is usually some element of protection wrapped in every rejection. This is a hard one to process at the time of the rejection. But for many of my past rejections, I can look back and see how God was allowing things to unfold the way they did for my protection.

In His mercy, He allowed this.

3. This is a short-term setback, not a permanent condition. The emotions that feel so intense today will ease up over time as long as we let them. We just have to watch how we think and talk about this rejection. If we give it the power to define us, it will haunt us long-term. But if we only allow it enough power to refine us, the hurt will give way to healing.

As I sat in that restaurant with Ashley and helped her process her fears through the filter of truth, courage emerged that no matter what happened—good or bad—she could trust God.

Finally, she clicked open the email revealing her grades. Not only did she pass; she was on the dean's list.

I was so thankful that day for tears of joy. But I'm also well aware that in the tomorrows that come, things could be different. Rejections big and small just seem to ebb and flow in and out of life. Troubles will probably still find us. But the Lord doesn't just deliver us from *some* of our troubles. Psalm 34:19 tells us He delivers us from them *all!*

And I'll give that truth a big, huge AMEN!

Father God, I don't understand this situation. But I do understand Your goodness to me. Help me replace the fears threatening to consume me with truth. I know You love me, You are for me, and I absolutely can trust You with all of my heart. In Jesus' Name, Amen.

68

THE BEST WORST THING

[Jesus] replied, "You of little faith, why are you so
afraid?" Then he got up and rebuked the winds
and the waves, and it was completely calm.
—MATTHEW 8:26

I failed at being a wedding planner.

No one wants a planner who gets so undone by the neurotic mother-of-the-bride that she throws up in the parking lot right beside the guest sidewalk.

Really, nothing says, "Welcome to my wedding" quite like that.

I failed at being a kitchen gadget saleswoman.

No one wants to see the tip of a thumb sliced off into the veggie pizza at the exact moment I was promising how safe this gadget is.

Awesome.

I failed at being a cafeteria lady at a private school.

My assistant decided her arms were so dry she needed to coat herself with our spray butter. When we took the trash out later that day, we both got attacked by bees and forgot about the pizza in the oven.

Kids don't take kindly to burnt pizza.

I failed at being a receptionist.

It's never a good idea to just succumb to those sleepy afternoon feelings and lay your head down on the desk.

Bosses don't like workers who snore. Even if they are pregnant.

Yes, I failed at a lot during those years when I was trying to figure out what to do with my life. At the time, each of these things felt like the worst that could have happened. Now, I think they were the *best worst things.*

> We live in a broken world full of broken people. But isn't it comforting to know God isn't ever broken?

Had these things been successful, I would have never discovered the joy of being in the ministry I'm in now.

I see this same theme woven throughout many stories in the Bible.

In Matthew 8:23–24 we find Jesus getting into a boat with His disciples. "Suddenly a furious storm came up on the lake, so that the waves swept over the boat." Worst thing.

But in verse 26 Jesus got up and rebuked the winds and waves and things turned completely calm. The disciples were amazed. *Best worst thing.*

In Acts 5:18 we find the apostles being arrested and thrown in jail. Worst thing.

But in Acts 5:19 we find an angel of the Lord opening the doors of the jail and bringing them out. Later we find them with so much confidence they boldly proclaim, "We must obey God rather than men" (v. 29 NASB). *Best worst thing.*

I don't understand why we have to go through cruddy stuff. And I certainly know there are many worse things to go through than what I've mentioned here.

We live in a broken world full of broken people. But isn't it comforting to know God isn't ever broken? He isn't ever caught off guard, taken by surprise, or shocked by what happens next.

He can take our worst and add His best. We just have to make the choice to stay with Him and keep following Him through it all.

Dear Lord, I know You are capable of taking my worst and turning it into Your best. Show me this truth anew today. Refresh my spirit. I want to follow You through it all. In Jesus' Name, Amen.

69

A Better Place to Park

Whatever is true, whatever is noble, whatever
is right, whatever is pure, whatever is lovely,
whatever is admirable—if anything is excellent
or praiseworthy—think about such things.
—Philippians 4:8

As I trace my fingers back across the timeline of my life, I can remember times when spiritual and emotional emptiness left me vulnerable. The shape of my lack was the absence of a biological father.

He took with him so much more than he ever could have imagined. Those few suitcases and plastic crates didn't just contain boxers, ties, old trophies, and dusty books. Somewhere in between his Old Spice and office files were shattered pieces of a little girl's heart.

Now I'm not a big fan of pointing to hurts from my childhood and saying, "All my issues can be linked back to what other people did to me. Let me cut open my hurts and wallow in all that leaks out." Everyone has hurts from their past. And everyone has the choice to either let those past hurts continue to haunt and damage them or to allow forgiveness to pave the way for us to be more compassionate toward others.

My dad's abandonment was so huge, so draining, that it caused me to fill my mind with only negative memories of him. In my mind, he never loved me at all.

And you know what? Maybe he didn't. But parking my mind only on negative thoughts about my dad left such a sadness in my heart. Though I've been touched by Jesus and my soul filled with God's good perspective and healing truths, there was still this very human part of me that felt so incredibly sad when I thought about what never was with my daddy.

Sometimes I could brush off this sadness with a little sigh and recitation of who I am in Christ. But other times it made me angry. And defensive. And deeply unsatisfied.

Then one day God surprised me in the most unusual way. While my dad still made no effort to connect with me, a sweet memory of him changed my dark perspective.

One winter I traveled to Vermont, where I woke up one morning to stare at what an overnight snowstorm had brought. I had never seen such snow in all my life. But what really caught my attention were the gigantic icicles hanging from the roof line. They were glorious.

As I stared out at them, suddenly a memory of my dad flashed across the screen of my mind.

I grew up in Florida, which meant no snow ever. But I remember praying for snow. Praying like a revival preacher at a tent meeting. If ever there could be snow in Florida, surely a passionate little girl's prayers could open up those heavenly storehouses where all snowflakes are kept.

One night the temperatures dropped surprisingly low and the weatherman called for a freeze, which was a rare thing

To dwell on hard things keeps us in hard spots.

in our area. How tragic there was no precipitation. It was the one night that snow might have been possible.

It broke my little snow bunny heart.

But the next morning I awoke to the most amazing sight. There were icicles everywhere. Gleaming, dripping, hanging, light-reflecting, glorious icicles were all over the trees in our backyard.

It was magical.

We were the only house on the block with this grand winter display.

Because I was the only girl whose daddy thought to intentionally put sprinklers out on the one night it froze.

I don't know where this memory had been hiding for too many years. But what a gift. Somewhere in the deep, mysterious, broken places of my dad's heart, there was an inkling of love.

While this certainly doesn't solve all the complications of being abandoned by my dad, it gives me a healthy thought to dwell on where he's concerned—one of those good thoughts the Bible tells us to think about: "Whatever is true, whatever is noble, whatever is right, whatever is pure, whatever is lovely, whatever is admirable—if anything is excellent or praiseworthy—think about such things" (Philippians 4:8). I like to call this "parking my mind in a better spot."

It's so easy to park our minds in bad spots. To dwell and rehash and wish things were different. But to dwell on hard things keeps us in hard spots and only serves to deepen our feelings of emotional emptiness.

This icicle memory gave me a new place to park.

Do you have something from your past that causes emotional emptiness? As a first step toward healing, ask the Lord to help you think of one thing good from this past situation or something good that has happened despite the pain.

Dear Lord, You know the hurts I have from the past that still drain me. Please show me a good place to park my mind when that pain stings me again. In Jesus' Name, Amen.

70

WISDOM TOGETHER

Who is wise and understanding among you? Let
them show it by their good life, by deeds done
in the humility that comes from wisdom.

—JAMES 3:13

For all of her life, this girl, my middle girl, has known a secret. When it all falls apart, there is a safe place. Her mom's arms. More than a hug, this place beats with the gentle rhythm of a heart that feels what she feels. So my girl brings what she can't bear to experience alone into this place. And we reconnect.

So, when my daughter crawled into my arms at the 3:00 a.m. hour a few years ago, I knew. Trouble had found its way into her heart. A boy, whom she thought would handle her heart gently, didn't. Her crush, crushed her.

She felt it all so deeply. And while I could see it was all for the best, I hurt for this girl with a split-open heart because she's mine—my girl who couldn't sleep so she slipped into my bed to be near the rhythmic heartbeat she's known since she was conceived.

And in the quiet middle of the night, I held her. I brushed her long brown hair off her tear-streaked face. I kissed the wet salt on her cheeks. And I whispered, "I love you."

And she knew I was safe. Her safe place to run and find when the world gets wild and cruel and heartbreakingly mean.

The next morning, she showed me the source of her middle-of-the-night anguish—a text message from him. His words were from a heart entangled with immaturity and his own sources of hurt. He's not a bad person. He was young. And sometimes young means incapable of handling situations the right way.

I understand that. Age has given me that gift. But my young girl did not understand. She took the words like daggers to the heart. And cried.

She handed me the phone.

"Help me reply."

There we sat in the midst of poached eggs and toast crumbs talking together, thinking together, replying together.

> *When we can rise up on the wisdom of others and get a new view of our situations, our next steps seem a little clearer.*

Together is a really good word. Together is what we need when we hit tough patches in life. No matter what hard place we find ourselves in, feeling alone can make us vulnerable to bad decisions. Hard places can so easily make us want to default to our feelings rather than to wisdom as our guide. That's not the best time to make a decision. Especially not alone.

I suspect if you're in a tough place, it probably feels more significant than a teenaged heartbreak. I understand. I've been there. And I'll probably be there again. And when we're there, we have to be honest that we're not in the place to make big decisions right then. Maybe we're not even in the place to make decisions on simple requests by others.

This doesn't make you bad or incapable. It makes you smart.

Smart enough to know to pause and take extra time when life takes on extenuating circumstances that are hard.

In this pause from decisions, go to your safe place. When the world beats you down, open up your Bible. Let His sentences finish yours. Let truth walk before you like a guide on a dark path.

And go also to someone in your sphere of influence whom you know is wise. How do we know whom to go to? The Bible makes it clear: "Who is wise and understanding among you? Let them show it by their good life, by deeds done in the humility that comes from wisdom" (James 3:13). Yes, let these wise people help you. Stand on top of their wisdom when you feel shaky with your own. When we can rise up on the wisdom of others and get a new view of our situations, our next steps seem a little clearer.

Father, please show me who is wise. Surround me with Your loving arms and the loving arms of Your people when I need them. In Jesus' Name, Amen.

71

WISDOM AND HUMILITY

When pride comes, then comes disgrace,
but with humility comes wisdom.
—PROVERBS 11:2

Often the people who have the most wisdom have experienced the most humility. Or sometimes even the most humiliation. A wisdom like none other can arise from those hard places that bring us low. Wisdom that's been unearthed in the messy, mud-puddle places of life. When this kind of wisdom sits in the heart of a person who is vulnerable enough to drop their pride and share what they know, that's a gift—a gift I desperately need when going through some stuff.

I'll never forget one year when I needed someone who had some of that hard-earned wisdom. One of my college-aged kids had done something that completely stunned me. And I was two days from leaving to speak at one of the biggest events of my life when I found out.

My first instinct was to cancel the trip. I curled up in my bed and cried.

I finally mustered up the energy to open my computer and figure out how to word my cancellation email. I had never canceled an event before, so I whispered a prayer asking God to please confirm He was okay with me canceling.

That's when I saw an email from my assistant telling me another speaker had canceled from this event and they were requesting I do two keynote messages. *Are you kidding me? I'm thinking I will not even be able to deliver one message, much less two!*

I knew I needed to stand on the wisdom from someone else who'd gone before me. Someone who had been through some stuff with her kids and still had to find the courage to speak.

So I called another speaker who I knew had some wisdom found in those places of humility and humiliation. It wasn't an easy call to make. I cringed at how raw and exposed this admission made me feel. But I knew I was safe with her because we'd had a conversation years ago where she shared some of the less-than-perfect dynamics in her family.

I called. And her words were a gift.

She was generous with her transparency. She assured me I wasn't alone with words like, "Me too," "I know," "We are going through our own hurts and disappointments even right now." There was not a drop of disgrace directed toward me in her voice. It was interesting that I'd read Proverbs 11:2 just that morning: "When pride comes, then comes disgrace, but with humility comes wisdom."

Yes, I knew from where her wisdom came.

She settled my wildly beating heart: "You're not alone, Lysa. The grace our audiences need is the same grace we must walk in daily. Let this hurt work for you, not against you. Go. You must go."

A wisdom like none other can arise from those hard places that bring us low.

I knew she was right. Wise. I stood on her wisdom and replied that I would do both keynotes. Then I called and informed my adult child that we were going to do this trip together.

We flew to the event together. We

walked through the hard place together. And in the midst of being humbled to the point of humiliation, I discovered my own hard-earned wisdom.

Wisdom is our silver lining. Wisdom will help us not repeat the mistakes we've made but rather grow stronger through them.

How do we find it? We come to the Lord and ask Him for it. We set aside our excuses, our habits, and our justifications, and whisper, "I need Your perspective, God. I come before You and humbly admit my desperate dependence on You."

Then we can start to understand what James was talking about when he instructs us to "consider it pure joy, my brothers and sisters, whenever you face trials of many kinds" (1:2). Doesn't that sound like a contradictory statement? Joy from trials? Until we realize he's telling us to "*consider it pure joy.*" In other words, through a lens of wisdom, look for joy in this unlikely place of trial. And then Scripture reveals the reason:

> Because you know that the testing of your faith produces perseverance. Let perseverance finish its work so that you may be mature and complete, not lacking anything. (vv. 3–4)

So, yes, I can now consider all this and find pure joy when I face trials. And I can gain wisdom in the midst of it all—wisdom I need, wisdom I can use to make even better decisions in the future, and wisdom others will need that I now have to give.

Dear Lord, thank You that You give us the silver lining of wisdom when we have hard times. Please bring into my life people I can learn from, and people to whom I can pass on the wisdom that I learn along the way. In Jesus' Name, Amen.

72

I'm Really Afraid

The angel of the LORD encamps around those
who fear him,
and he delivers them.
—PSALM 34:7

A few years ago, one of my back teeth started hurting. It wasn't the first time that tooth had given me trouble, and quite honestly, I just didn't want to deal with it. That tooth had been a complete pain. Literally.

I'd had not one, not two, but three crowns done on the same tooth. The first one broke. The second one broke. And though the third one seemed like it would finally work, the tooth started aching again. Ugh!

The dentist informed me the only thing to do was to have a root canal.

I'm okay with the word *root*. And I'm okay with the word *canal*. But when he put those two words together a wild fear whipped its tentacles around my heart and squeezed the life out of me. I couldn't do it. I just couldn't bring myself to schedule the appointment.

So I dealt with the throbbing pain.

For a year, I didn't chew on that side of my mouth. I didn't let cold drinks leak over to that side. And I took ibuprofen when the throbbing got the best of me.

A year!

Finally I'd had enough. The pain overrode the fear, and I made an appointment for the dreaded root canal.

And you know what? I survived! Not only did I survive, but I honestly found the whole root canal ordeal to be no big deal. The fear of it was so much worse than actually having the procedure done.

I think fear often plays out that way. Sometimes living in fear of what might be causes more stress and anxiety than actually facing what we fear. Is there something you're avoiding because you're afraid?

Sometimes living in fear of what might be causes more stress and anxiety than actually facing what we fear.

Psalm 34:7 reminds me, "The angel of the Lord encamps around those who fear him, and he delivers them." To fear the Lord means to honor Him and magnify Him in my heart most of all. When I focus on or magnify my fears, they become all I can think about. So instead I've learned to focus on God by doing three things:

I cry out to Him with honest prayers. I verbalize to God what I'm afraid of and how paralyzing my fear is. I ask Him to help me see if this fear is a warning or an unnecessary worry. And then I ask Him to help me know the next step to take.

I open my Bible and look for verses that show me what He wants me to do in that moment of fear. I write down truths from the Bible about fear and then align my next thoughts and actions with His truth.

I then *walk in the assurance that I am fearing (honoring) the Lord* as Psalm 34:7 tells me to, therefore I know with certainty an angel of the Lord is encamped around me, and God will deliver me.

I like this promise so much. It comforts me. It reassures me. And it challenges me to really live like I know it is true.

What's a fear you can face today? Think of an everyday fear holding you back. Is there a fear of confronting an issue with a friend? Is there a fear of stepping out in obedience to something God is calling you to do? Is there a fear of a medical diagnosis you just received?

Oh, if I were there, I would totally hold your hand. Better yet, though, God is with you. And He is holding you. And when you know He is with you and His angels are encamped around you, you can face your fears.

Dear Lord, if a feeling of fear is a legitimate warning from You, help me to know that. But if this feeling of fear is more of a distracting detriment, help me be courageous and walk assured in Your presence. In Jesus' Name, Amen.

73

HOLDING ON TO TRUTH

"Then you will know the truth, and
the truth will set you free."
—JOHN 8:32

Several years ago I was wrapping up at a conference where I'd been speaking. My friend Beth and I were talking about where the team would be meeting for dinner that night when, suddenly, a very frantic arena staff member came over and told us there was an emergency and we were needed right away.

A lady attending the conference had just been told her two grandchildren had been killed in a fire that day.

We rushed over to find a lady surrounded by her friends. She was sobbing to the point she could hardly breathe. She'd just been with her grandbabies, ages eight and four. They'd spent spring break with her the week before. She'd held them, rocked them, stroked their hair, and kissed them all over their faces. How could they be gone?

It was too much for her brain to process.

The EMT stepped aside so we could hold her hands and pray over her. At first I stumbled my way through requests for Jesus to pour His most tender mercies into this situation. I prayed for comfort and the reassurance that these children were being held by Jesus in this moment.

Our souls were formed to recognize and respond to the calm assurance of Jesus.

It was so hard. My mommy heart ached so deeply for this woman. My eyes welled up with tears refusing to stay contained.

As Beth took her turn to pray I noticed something miraculous. Every time we said "Jesus," her body calmed, her crying slowed, her breathing stopped sounding so panicked.

So, when it was my turn to pray again I just said His name over and over and over. This sweet grandmother joined me, "Jesus, Jesus, Jesus."

As we said "Jesus" over and over, truth flooded my mind.

I remembered what I'd discovered in Scripture about fearing death. Death is only a temporary separation. We will be reunited again.

I remembered truth from 2 Samuel 12. When David's infant child died, David confidently said, "I will go to him, but he will not return to me" (v. 23). David knew he would see his child again—not just a nameless, faceless soul without an identity, but his very child. He would know him, hold him, kiss him, and the separation death caused would be over.

The only thing that seemed to calm my devastated sister in Christ was the name of Jesus and His truth.

What a powerful reminder to us all.

Hold on to His Word, sweet sister. Speak His truth and the name of Jesus out loud. Our souls were formed to recognize and respond to the calm assurance of Jesus and truth.

Never has this been clearer to me.

Please pray for my friend from the conference and her family.

And remember no matter what circumstances you find yourself in . . .

We can choose to hold on to the truth. Let everything else go. Park our mind with what is true. "Then you will know the truth, and the truth will set you free" (John 8:32).

Dear Lord, I lift up my mind to You and ask You to help me remember to speak Your Name and Your truth in any situation I'm in that seems overwhelming—little things and big things. Truly my soul was formed to recognize and respond to the calm assurance of truth. In Jesus' Name, Amen.

74

PRESSING THROUGH THE PAIN

Draw near to God and He will draw near to you.
—JAMES 4:8 (NKJV)

*D*oes it ever feel like the heartbreak in your life is trying to break you? I understand. I really, really do. I've been in that place where the pain of heartbreak hits with such sudden and sharp force that it feels like it cuts through skin and bone. It's the kind of pain that leaves us wondering if we'll ever be able to function like a normal person again.

But God has been tenderly reminding me that pain itself is not the enemy. Pain is the indicator that brokenness exists.

Pain is the reminder that the real Enemy is trying to take us out and bring us down by keeping us stuck in broken places. Pain is the gift that motivates us to fight with brave tenacity and fierce determination, knowing there's healing on the other side.

And in the in-between? In that desperate place where we aren't quite on the other side of it all yet, and our heart still feels quite raw?

Pain is the invitation for God to move in and replace our faltering strength with His. I'm not writing that to throw out spiritual platitudes that sound good; I write it from the depth of a heart that knows it's the only way.

We must invite God into our pain to help us survive the desperate in-between.

The only other choice is to run from the pain by using some method of numbing. But numbing the pain never goes to the source of the real issue to make us healthier. It only silences our screaming need for help.

If we avoid the hurt, the hurt creates a void in us.

We think we are freeing ourselves from the pain when, in reality, what numbs us imprisons us. If we avoid the hurt, the hurt creates a void in us. It slowly kills the potential for our hearts to fully feel, fully connect, fully love again. It even steals the best in our relationship with God.

Pain is the sensation that indicates a transformation is needed. There is a weakness where new strength needs to enter in. And we must choose to pursue long-term strength rather than temporary relief.

So how do we get this new strength? How do we stop ourselves from chasing what will numb us when the deepest parts of us scream for some relief? How do we stop the piercing pain of this minute, this hour?

We invite God's closeness.

For me, this means praying. No matter how vast our pit, prayer is big enough to fill us with the realization of His presence like nothing else. Our key verse (James 4:8) reminds us that when we draw near to God, He will draw near to us. When we invite Him close, He always accepts our invitation.

And on the days when my heart feels hurt and my words feel quite flat, I let Scripture guide my prayers—recording His Word in my journal, and then adding my own personal thoughts.

One of my favorites to turn to is Psalm 91. I would love to share this verse with you today, as an example for when you prayerfully invite God into your own pain.

Verse: "Whoever dwells in the shelter of the Most High will rest in the shadow of the Almighty" (Psalm 91:1).

Prayer:

Lord, draw me close.

Your Word promises when I draw close to You, You are there. I want my drawing close to be a permanent dwelling place. At any moment when I feel weak and empty and alone, I pray that I won't let those feelings drag me down into a pit of insecurity. But rather, I want those feelings to be triggers for me to immediately lift those burdensome feelings to You and trade them for the assurance of Your security.

I am not alone, because You are with me. I am not weak, because Your strength is infused in me. I am not empty, because I'm drinking daily from Your fullness. You are my dwelling place. And in You I have shelter from every stormy circumstance and harsh reality. I'm not pretending the hard things don't exist, but I am rejoicing in the fact that Your covering protects me and prevents those hard things from affecting me like they used to.

You, the Most High, have the final say over me. You know me and love me intimately. And today I declare that I will trust You in the midst of my pain. You are my everyday dwelling place, my saving grace. In Jesus' Name, Amen.

And with that I close my prayer journal, feeling a lot less desperate and a lot more whole. I breathe the atmosphere of life His words bring.

I picture Him standing at the door of my future, knocking. If I will let Him enter into the darkness of my hurt today, He will open wide the door to a much brighter tomorrow.

Dear Lord, in this moment I draw near to You and I invite Your closeness. Help me to experience Your presence today. In Jesus' Name, Amen.

75

DEVASTATED BUT NOT DESTROYED

He says, "Be still, and know that I am God;
I will be exalted among the nations,
I will be exalted in the earth."
—PSALM 46:10

I took my seat in the middle of the food court and was thankful I could hide my tears by staring down at my food. I quietly brushed my napkin across my cheek. I blinked. I tried desperately to swallow.

I'm not normally a mall-goer, but that day I needed a place to hide. A place to process. A place to remember that the whole world wasn't falling apart.

The news I'd received just an hour earlier crushed me. And devastated me.

A friend I love made a decision that I couldn't for the life of me understand. It wasn't in keeping with her character. It wasn't something I ever dreamed this person could do. The effects of this decision would careen across her life and mine with really hard consequences.

Glancing at the table across from me I saw two women a little younger than me. They were laughing and cutting up food into bite-size pieces for their young kids. I could hear them talking about costumes that needed to be made for their upcoming preschool performance. One of them was having a hard time finding purple tights

God loves us
and He will
not leave us.

and she desperately needed purple tights to make the costume complete.

I whispered under my breath, "I wish my biggest issue was purple tights." Although my whispered statement was lost in the chaotic chorus of food court voices and noises, the scream inside my heart hovered over me in deafening tones.

What. In. The. World!

My mind raced. My throat tightened. My eyes leaked uncontrollably.

I tried to pray but honestly I felt like God was pretty distant at that moment.

It's hard to stand on the goodness of God when you feel like life has just been stripped of so much good.

I forced my legs to support my body. I walked mindlessly to my car. And I drove home.

It's in these moments when we know if the Word of God has seeped deep into our hearts or not. Though the world seemed to swirl and spin without anything for me to hold onto, one simple statement rose to the top of my mind and cut through with crystal clarity, "Be still, and know that I am God" (Psalm 46:10).

I heard it over and over.

And I knew it wasn't my mind conjuring up this Bible verse. It was the Holy Spirit inside me speaking. Reassuring. And quite honestly, holding me together when circumstances were tearing me apart.

I don't know what hard reality is crushing your heart right now. But I sense I'm not alone. The Enemy is on a full-out attack against everything good, sacred, pure, and honest. He is the father of lies who wants us to believe that if our circumstances fall apart, then so will we.

But take it from a woman in the middle of my own hard reality: Satan is a liar. God is a Redeemer. A Healer. The Author of hope. The Pathway of restoration. The great I AM.

Right this very minute there are some things you and I must cling and hold to as if our lives depended on it:

1. God loves us and He will not leave us.
2. This battle isn't ours. The battle belongs to the Lord. Let Him fight for you. Save your emotional energy and use it to dig into His Word like never before. Our job is to be obedient to God. God's job is winning this battle.
3. The battle might not be easy or short-lived, but victory will be there for those who trust God.
4. God is good even when the circumstances are darker than you ever imagined. God is good even when people are not. God is good even when things seem stinking hopeless. God is good and can be trusted when you feel suspicious of everyone and everything around you.
5. Lastly, God is good at being God. Don't try to fix what He hasn't assigned you to fix. Don't try to manipulate or control or spend all your emotions trying to figure it out. Let Him be God. Free yourself from this impossible assignment.

Sweet friend, be still. And know. He is God.

I'm praying for you. And I treasure the fact I know you are praying for me.

Let's band together to declare we Jesus girls may not have all the answers for our situations. But by God we will stand in the midst of our hard days and declare we trust the One who holds every answer.

We will . . . be still . . . and know . . . HE IS GOD.

Dear Lord, I choose to hand my situation over to You today. I will be still and know that You, and only You, are God. In Jesus' Name, Amen.

Part 4

Embracing His Call to Be Transformed

76

THE BEGINNINGS OF A MIRACLE

I will remember the deeds of the LORD;
yes, I will remember your miracles of long ago.
—PSALM 77:11

*I*f I lived in the days of Jesus, I like to think I'd have been moved by His miracles. Changed by His miracles. Repentant and willing to live differently because of what His actions proved. He is the Son of God—the miracle worker.

But would I really?

After all, sometimes I act as though Jesus can work miracles for other people, but not for me. Not with my issues.

A few years ago, I started to see that one of my issues was my short and snippy reactions to my family. I felt like I was constantly coming unglued and getting all tangled in my raw emotions. I chalked it up to stress, being overly tired, and monthly hormonal fluxes. I kept making excuses and promises to do better tomorrow. But then tomorrow would bring with it more challenges and conflicts where I'd overreact again and then regret it.

I was quick to applaud when other people repented and positioned their hearts to see Jesus work miracles in their lives. But I lived as if that same kind of miraculous work wasn't possible with me.

And that kind of unrepentant attitude frustrates Jesus. In Matthew

11:20, "Jesus began to denounce the towns in which most of his miracles had been performed, because they did not repent."

Sometimes I have to get out of my normal surroundings to become more aware of things that need to change in me. So, that year I spent a week at a homeless shelter called the Dream Center. Pastor Matthew Barnett and his church run the Dream Center in Los Angeles. The Dream Center is a ministry hub of programs that serves thousands of people each month who are dealing with the heartbreaking effects of homelessness, addiction, sex trafficking, and more.

I knew my progress would be imperfect, but it could still be miraculous.

I went to help meet needs. But I quickly realized I was there as a woman in need. A woman who needed God's reality to fall fresh and heavy and close and real and too in my face to deny.

I saw God's miraculous healing power woven into so many lives at the Dream Center. I saw it. And wanted it.

God's miraculous power is what transformed the gang member with eight bullet-hole scars into a Jesus-loving servant. So gentle.

It's what changed the former prostitute into a counselor for other girls rescued from life on the streets. So pure.

It's what changed the drug addict into a loving father, teaching his son how to be a godly leader. So integrity filled.

What prevented me from realizing that God's power could change me too?

Somewhere along the line I stopped *expecting* God to work miraculously in me.

The psalmist in our key verse stirred his soul to hope by remembering the miracles of the Lord: "I will remember the deeds of the LORD; yes, I will remember your miracles of long ago" (Psalm 77:11). And I realized I could do the same thing. Inspired by the changed lives at the homeless shelter, my soul quickened to the bold reality that I could be different. I really could have different reactions to my raw emotions. I knew my progress would be imperfect, but it could still be miraculous. And I felt a new hope rush through me.

I'm not gentle by nature, but I can be gentle by obedience. I'm not patient by nature, but I can be patient by obedience. I'm not peaceful by nature, but I can be peaceful by obedience.

I can. And I will.

I can be the unglued woman made gentle, patient, and peaceful. God, help me. God, forgive me. And in the shadow of that realization and repentance, the miracle begins.

Dear Lord, please open my eyes to see the places I need You to change in me. I know I have wrapped my identity in so many things other than You. I want You to change those rough, imperfect places in me. Help me become the woman You created me to be. In Jesus' Name, Amen.

77

IS MY PAIN TALKING?

We take captive every thought to make it obedient to Christ.
—2 CORINTHIANS 10:5

*S*ometimes something *little* can feel really *big*. A look from someone
that suddenly made you feel like they didn't like you. Or someone
doesn't return your phone call and you feel like it's an indication that
you're not important.

Usually these things aren't true.

The look was just a look with no hidden meaning.

The missed phone call was just a slip on that person's to-do list.

But if we're not careful, those misguided feelings can create issues
that distract us, discourage us, and trigger past pain that starts taunting us. They can fill our minds with thoughts that are not accurate.

It happened to me on the Friday after Thanksgiving. My sister
Angee and I got up at 3:00 a.m. and were in line at a store thirty minutes
later. I know. I agree. That's crazy.

But like a hunter stalking prey, I was after something. In this case,
the buy-one-get-one-free washer and dryer. Angee was after a half-
priced computer. When the store doors opened at 5:00 a.m., we both
scored. Happiness abounded. Then we left to get some breakfast.
This is the part of the story where the happiness faded.

In the drive-through, my credit card was "not approved."

Let me get this straight. It was approved at the store just five minutes ago when I made a major purchase. But now for a little two-dollar bundle of egg, cheese, Canadian bacon, and an English muffin, suddenly I'm not approved?

Not approved.

Ouch.

My sister wasn't fazed. She whipped out cash, paid for my breakfast, and headed to the next store on our list. But I let those words "not approved" hang like a black cloud over my head. It bothered the stink out of me. I knew it was just some technical glitch, but I let my mind dwell on it until it was no longer about the card.

When that girl leaned out of the drive-thru window and in a hushed tone said, "I'm sorry, ma'am, but your card keeps showing that you're not approved," it felt personal. Really personal.

Suddenly, past pain from other times I'd felt rejected and my current embarrassment started running their mouth inside my head. *You're nothing but a loser. You are unwanted. Unloved. Disorganized. Poor. Not acceptable. You are not approved.*

I wish I could tie up this story in a nice bow and give you a pretty ending, but I can't. It was anything but pretty. I felt awful. And I went to bed wondering if the Lord Himself might come down and say, "Lysa TerKeurst, I have had enough of your immature reactions. You are no longer approved to be a Bible study teacher. Look at you!"

But that's not the Lord's voice. Our Lord doesn't whisper shameful condemnations.

> *Our Lord doesn't whisper shameful condemnations. Spiritual convictions, yes. Personal condemnations, no.*

Spiritual convictions, yes. Personal condemnations, no.

As I stared wide-eyed into the darkness that enveloped the room, I whispered, "Give me Your voice, Jesus. I need to hear You above all these painful thoughts. If I don't hear You, I'm afraid this darkness is going to swallow me alive." Nothing came. I couldn't hear a thing.

I had a choice. I could lie in the dark replaying the awful events of the day, or I could turn the light on and read God's Word—His truth—which is the best thing to do when lies are swarming and painful thoughts are attacking like a bunch of bloodthirsty mosquitoes. It is choosing to do what 2 Corinthians 10:5 encourages us to do—take every thought to Jesus and let Him correct or redirect it with the truth of his Word.

Lies flee in the presence of truth. Comfort comes into our pain when we bring it to Jesus. And while reading God's truth that night didn't change the fact that I needed to make things right in my thoughts, it gave me the courage to do so.

Dear Lord, please drown out the other voices . . . please hush the negative thoughts . . . and speak. I want to hear You above all the noise. Help me discern Your convictions and the Devil's condemnations. In Jesus' Name, Amen.

78

GETTING UNSTUCK FROM MY THINKING RUT

Do not conform to the pattern of this world, but be
transformed by the renewing of your mind. Then
you will be able to test and approve what God's
will is—his good, pleasing and perfect will.

—ROMANS 12:2

*H*ave you felt discouraged with your progress toward having better reactions? Maybe you think, *What's the use? I just stuff my emotions.* Or, *What's the use? I can't help but yell.*

Sweet friend, I believe there is more to it than claiming that because we act a certain way, that's the way it will always be.

Brain research shows that every conscious thought we have is recorded on our internal hard drive known as the cerebral cortex. Each thought scratches the surface much like an Etch A Sketch.

When we have the same thought again, the line of the original thought is deepened, causing what's called a memory trace. With each repetition the trace goes deeper and deeper, forming and embedding a pattern of thought. When an emotion is tied to this thought pattern, the memory trace grows exponentially stronger.

We forget most of our random thoughts that are not tied to an emotion. However, we retain the ones we think often that have

If we change the way we think, we'll change the ways we act and react.

an emotion tied to them. For example, if we've had the thought over and over that we've failed at having a good reaction, and that thought is tied to a strong emotion, we deepen the memory trace when we repeatedly access that thought. The same is true if we decide to stuff a thought—we'll perpetuate that stuffing. Or if we yell, we'll keep yelling.

We won't develop new responses until we develop new thoughts. That's why renewing our minds with new thoughts is crucial. New thoughts come from new perspectives. The Bible encourages this process, which only makes sense because God created the human mind and understands better than anyone how it functions.

A foundational teaching of Scripture is that it is possible to be completely changed through transformed thought patterns. That's exactly the point of today's key verse, Romans 12:2: "Do not conform to the pattern of this world, but be transformed by the renewing of your mind. Then you will be able to test and approve what God's will is—his good, pleasing and perfect will."

And, as we learned yesterday, Scripture also teaches that we can accept or refuse thoughts. Instead of being held hostage by old thought patterns, we can actually capture our thoughts and allow the power of Christ's truth to change them.

I don't know about you, but understanding how my brain is designed makes these verses come alive in a whole new way. Taking thoughts captive and being transformed by thinking in new ways isn't some New Age form of mind control. It's biblical, and it's fitting with how God wired our brains.

I can't control the things that happen to me each day, but I can control how I think about them. I can say to myself, *I have a choice to have destructive thoughts or constructive thoughts right now. I can wallow in what's wrong and make things worse, or I can ask God for a better perspective to help me see good even when I don't feel good.*

Indeed, when we gain new perspectives, we can see new ways of thinking. And if we change the way we think, we'll change the ways we act and react.

Dear Lord, teach me to trust You and to believe that even though my situation is overwhelming, You always have the best for me in mind. Give me Your perspective today. In Jesus' Name, Amen.

79

THE ROOT OF MY ROT

Point out anything in me that offends you,
and lead me along the path of everlasting life.
—PSALM 139:24 NLT

Recently, a friend of mine hurt my feelings and I got all bent out of shape. And, honey, everyone in my house knew Mama wasn't happy. I tried everything to usher gentleness back into my tone and my temper.

I quoted verses.

I rebuked Satan.

I bossed my feelings around with truth.

I even tried to take a nap.

But none of these activities soothed me.

What really sent me over the edge, though, was a smell that started to fill my home that not even three strongly scented candles could mask.

Unfortunately, as the mysterious, awful smell continued to waft through my home, I couldn't for the life of me figure out what it was or where it was coming from.

Finally, I realized my daughter had placed a trash can in the middle of my bedroom floor so she could toss scraps of paper as she worked on a school project. Some food had obviously been thrown away in that forgotten trash can that had surpassed gross and moved into the final stages of rot.

I didn't have the heart to find out what the rot was; I just knew the trash can had to go. Immediately.

The smell was an outside indication of an internal situation. And the trash can wasn't the only thing that stunk that night. So did my attitude.

My reaction was also an outside indication of an internal situation.

The reason I couldn't be soothed by quoting Scripture, bossing my feelings, rebuking Satan, or even taking a nap is because God wanted me to be aware of my stink . . . something inside of me that stunk . . . a place starting to rot.

How we react is a crucial gauge of what's really going on inside us.

I'd been hurt by a friend and didn't want to confront the issue or forgive the person who had hurt me. I'd stuffed bitterness in my heart and tried to pretend it wasn't there. But the rot was there and the stink from deep within my heart kept spilling out.

God didn't want me to temporarily mask the situation by feeling better in the moment. He wanted me to address the root of my rot—to see it, admit it, expose it, let Him clean it up, and shut it down. Immediately.

Psalm 139:24 reminds us of King David's plea to the Lord: "Point out anything in me that offends you, and lead me along the path of everlasting life." We must have this same attitude when it comes to our own lives.

A little rot can spread fast and furiously if not dealt with swiftly and seriously. That's why it's so crucial to pay attention to our reactions today.

How we react is a crucial gauge of what's really going on inside us.

When people or issues or situations bump into our happy, it's not wrong to feel annoyed. But if that annoyance leads to a reaction out of proportion to the issue at hand, we can bank on the fact that this eruption has a root of rot.

Here are some telltale signs of roots of rot:

- I throw out statements like, "You always . . . You never . . . Why can't we ever . . ."
- I start gathering ammunition from past situations to build my case.
- I use words and a tone outside my normal character.
- I justify my reaction by pointing out how hard my life is right now.
- I demand an apology, all the while knowing I should be giving one.

These are not fun to admit, but here's the beauty of the situation: The quicker we see a root of rot, the quicker we can get rid of the stink and move forward.

Dear Lord, thank You for bringing to light the rotting areas of my life. Help me address these areas with Your grace and truth. In Jesus' Name, Amen.

I Quit

*Godly sorrow brings repentance that leads to salvation
and leaves no regret, but worldly sorrow brings death.*
—2 Corinthians 7:10

My heart is stirred today to say it's time to quit.

Not ministry.

Not a diet or an exercise plan.

But quit being critical of a friend I love very much. The crazy thing is, I'm not a critical person. But I've found myself slipping into a pattern of giving this person what they give me.

They criticize.

So, I've started criticizing back. A lot.

And I'm feeling very convicted today that I need to model a different attitude and approach to life.

Recently, my pastor said something very convicting in his sermon. He said, "Jesus didn't die so we'd be sorry. He died and then He was resurrected so we'd be changed."

Changed.

There is a big difference between being sorry and being changed.

To be sorry means to feel bad. It's a temporary little prick of the heart.

But change only comes when we're repentant. Being repentant is a deeper conviction to correct and transform our behavior—our habit—our wrong tendency.

In 2 Corinthians 7:10 we learn, "Godly sorrow brings repentance that leads to salvation and leaves no regret, but worldly sorrow leads to death." *Leaves no regret*—those are powerful words.

I want to live a life of no regrets.

And I think today is a really good day to address something that could lead to a big ol' pile of regret.

So, each time I'm feeling the need to criticize I'm going to see it as a call to flip my words to encouragement.

There is a big difference between being sorry and being changed.

I might still need to address some issues with this person but I will do it by pointing out their strengths and the responsibilities that come with those strengths rather than constantly focusing on their weaknesses.

For example: "You are an influencer! Have you noticed when you are happy others are happy but when you are negative it really affects those around you? I need your help to keep things positive today. Do you think you can accept this leadership role? How can you be a positive influence in this situation?"

I'm not naive enough to think this will be easy. I will need grace. They will need grace. But at least if I'm aware of how I need to change, change can be set in motion.

Are you up for quitting some old habit, negative attitude, or wrong tendency? I know I am. The next time we're presented with an opportunity, let's remember the words of my pastor, "Jesus didn't die so we'd be sorry. He died and then He was resurrected so we'd be changed."

Dear Lord, I'm ready to quit. Instead of critical words, I want to speak kind and encouraging ones. Will You please help me make this shift? In Jesus' Name, Amen.

Receiving Grace

I will bless the Lord at all times: his praise
shall continually be in my mouth.
—Psalm 34:1 kjv

I couldn't even blame this one on hormones. It was just too much, happening too fast, in too condensed of a time period, with too many people determined to get on my last good nerve.

I'll give it to you in two-word snippets. And while I'm running down my list, see if any empathy starts to find its way to your heart. Because I'm convinced if there is one way all us girls are alike, it's in the reality that life isn't always so pretty.

Computer crash. Birthday forgotten. Whiny child. Stained pants. Pounds gained. Feelings hurt. Tempers short. Dog fleas. Pantry ants. Throbbing head. Interrupted nap. Sibling spat. Time out. Messy car. Gas prices. Urgent errands. No time. Doctor appointment. Waiting room. Waiting room. Waiting room. Misplaced belonging. Futile search. Hand wringing. Messy kitchen. Chores undone. Laundry piles. Paper piles. Dinner flop. Early bedtime.

Sheer exhaustion.

And yes, all that and more happened on my birthday. And all the girlfriends sighed a unified, "Have mercy."

I really wish I could put a godly spin on how I reacted in these situations. I would love to share how I smiled and remained calm and didn't yell at those I love and didn't pout about the forgotten birthday. I would love to be able to say I took the high road and handled everything with grace as my little halo shined.

In the midst of my mess, God is there.

But I'm afraid only one word describes my overall attitude: *ugly*. And when my ugly comes out, I am so often tempted to think God leaves me. I wouldn't blame Him. Who wouldn't want to get away from someone with an ungrateful heart and a stinky attitude?

But God is too full of grace to walk away. Grace doesn't give me a free pass to act out how I feel, with no regard for His commands. Rather His grace gives me consolation in the moment, with a challenge to learn from this situation and become more mature in the future.

Grace is the sugar that helps the bitter pills of confession and repentance go down without choking. That's why the writer of Hebrews says, "Let us then approach the throne of grace with confidence, so that we may receive mercy and find grace to help us in our time of need" (Hebrews 4:16). Grace is the reason I can go to God quickly, immediately—*before* I'm cleaned up—and boldly ask for His help. In the midst of my mess, God is there.

When I am short-tempered and flat-out grumpy, I often don't feel God. But the reality is, He is with me. All I have to do to sense His presence is to acknowledge His presence, ask for His help, and make the choice to praise Him despite my feelings.

Though praise is not often the first or even the tenth thing we naturally think about when the messy realities of life hit, if we keep praise in the forefront of our minds it will become easier and easier to make that choice. Just like any other discipline, practicing it over and over will help it to become more natural. I can become a woman whose heart declares, "I will bless the Lord at all times: his praise shall continually be in my mouth."

No, life isn't always pretty. That's a given. But we can have a glimmer of hope that it is possible to make wise choices with our thoughts, actions, and reactions. These choices involve getting honest with ourselves and learning—sometimes over and over—the power of praise. Especially when the uglies come knocking.

Lord, thank You that You are with me—even when my ugly side comes out, even when I'm a mess, even when I don't feel You with me. Thank You for Your grace, Your help, and Your forgiveness. In Jesus' Name, Amen.

THE TREASURE OF THROWN-AWAY FOOD

The peace of God, which transcends all understanding,
will guard your hearts and your minds in Christ Jesus.
—PHILIPPIANS 4:7

few years ago, my son Jackson wrote a paper about the corruption and greed that caused the civil war in his native land. But Jackson wasn't just explaining a historical event—he and his brother Mark lived in the midst of the horrific conditions of this war. You see, for the early years of their lives, my sons lived in a forgotten orphanage in the third world country of Liberia, Africa.

During one part of the paper, Jackson described what it felt like to be naked digging through the trash looking for the treasure of thrown-away food.

The treasure of thrown-away food.

I can hardly type those words without crying. This is my son.

And yet, despite the horrific conditions of his childhood, there was an unexplainable thread of peace woven through his recollection of the story. A powerful peace centered in the awareness of God's presence.

The truly thankful person is a truly peaceful person. They have made a habit, no matter what, to notice, pause, and choose.

Noticing something for which to be thankful no matter their circumstance.

Pausing to acknowledge this something as a reminder of God's presence.

Choosing to focus on God's presence until His powerful peace is unleashed.

Will we be a noticer? A pauser? A chooser? A person of thanksgiving no matter what circumstance we're facing?

I find this truth about the power of thanksgiving over and over in Scripture. What was the prayer Daniel prayed right before being thrown in the lion's den and witnessing God miraculously shutting the lion's mouths? Thanksgiving.

After three days in the belly of a fish, what was the cry of Jonah's heart right before he was finally delivered onto dry land? Thanksgiving.

> *The truly thankful person is a truly peaceful person.*

How are we instructed to pray in Philippians 4:6 when we feel anxious? With thanksgiving.

And what is the outcome of each of these situations where thanksgiving is proclaimed? Peace.

Powerful, unexplainable, uncontainable peace.

"The peace of God, which transcends all understanding, will guard your hearts and your minds in Christ Jesus" (Philippians 4:7).

One of Webster's official definitions of thanksgiving is, "a public acknowledgment or celebration of divine goodness."

I wonder how we might celebrate God's divine goodness today.

I wonder what might happen if we decide in the midst of our circumstances today to notice, pause, and choose something for which we can truly be thankful.

Dear Lord, will You help me notice things for which I can be thankful in each circumstance I face today? Will You help me remember to pause and acknowledge this as evidence of Your presence? And will You help me remember to choose to focus on Your presence until Your powerful peace rushes into my heart and helps me see everything more clearly? Thank You for the reality that being thankful changes everything. In Jesus' Name, Amen.

83

GIVING GRACE

Our struggle is not against flesh and blood, but
against the rulers, against the authorities, against
the powers of this dark world and against the
spiritual forces of evil in the heavenly realms.

—EPHESIANS 6:12

I woke up one morning in a twit. I don't know what the official definition of a twit is. Nor am I completely sure twit is a real word.
However, when you feel all twisted up with irritation sprinkled on top,
twit seems fitting.

So, there I was in a twit on a new day.

Typically, I am a pretty gentle person. But on this day I could envi-
sion myself saying the perfect comeback to this person who hurt me
and it felt good. I mentally weighed out all the many reasons I was
perfectly justified in leveling the scales of hurt.

They dumped a bucket of hurt on me. The scale tipped heavy on
my side.

Therefore, I should dump a bucket of hurt on them. Then the
scales would be even and my twit would dissipate in this balance of
hurt equality.

But something in my spirit didn't feel better after I mentally
walked through this leveling of the scales.

I felt heavy.

And that's when it occurred to me.

> *The secret to healthy conflict resolution isn't taking a you-against-me-stance, but realizing it's all of us against Satan— he's the real Enemy.*

In God's economy, people don't stand on opposing sides of the conflict scale. People stand on one side and Satan stands on the other. When we dump hurt into one another's lives, we aren't leveling the conflict scale. We are just making the people side fall further and further while Satan's side becomes more and more elevated.

Satan loves when we do his work for him by dumping on each other.

The secret to healthy conflict resolution isn't taking a "you against me" stance. The secret is realizing it's "us against Satan." He's the real Enemy here. In Ephesians 6:12 Paul reminds us that our struggle is not against flesh and blood but against the spiritual forces of evil in the heavenly realms.

But this is hard when all we see is that flesh-and-blood person standing there who quite honestly has managed to get on the last good nerve we have left.

This moment may seem like the perfect time to set our Christianity on the shelf.

In actuality though, moments of conflict are hands down the grandest opportunity to shame Satan back to hell.

When a Jesus girl rises up and gives unexpected gentle grace when she surely could have done an attitude cuss, the mystery of Christ is seen more clearly than ever.

That's why Paul ends Ephesians 6 with a charge regarding our words.

After telling us in verse 12 that Satan is our real Enemy, reminding us to put on our spiritual armor each day, and reiterating the absolute necessity of prayer, He says one more thing. "Pray that whenever I open my mouth, words may be given me so that I will fearlessly make known the mystery of the gospel" (v. 19).

The placement of this verse is crucial and intentional. What a choice we have to make.

Father, help me remember who my Enemy really is—and that You give me grace to pass along to others. In Jesus' Name, Amen.

84

SOMETHING TO CONSIDER WITH CRITICISM

Criticism is awful. That's usually my first thought when a friend, family member, or even an acquaintance makes it clear they don't like something I've done or said.

My pride says, "How dare you!"

My heart says, "I want a chance to explain."

My soul says, "Jesus, am I off base?"

My mind says, "Why do I open myself up like this?"

My feelings say, "Ouch."

Sometimes criticism is fair. Maybe I messed up and it would serve me well to reconsider. Other times criticism is nothing but rotten spew. And boy, does it stink. But if I get stuck in the stink, it serves no good purpose.

Might there be another way to look at harsh criticism? Is there a way to get past the hurt to see something about the one criticizing me that will soften my heart toward them?

Recently, I stumbled on an article about the armadillo lizard. This fascinating creature has hard and pointy scales that have "Don't mess with me" written all over them. But, like all tough creatures, this lizard has a vulnerable place.

The armadillo lizard's tough exterior wraps around its back but softens at the underbelly. When threatened, the lizard grabs its tail and displays a prickly, intimidating posture to keep other creatures away. At that point, the rest of the body serves only one purpose—to hide and protect its most vulnerable part.

So what does a strange desert creature have to do with criticism?

In an effort to protect my underbelly, I sometimes get all wrapped up in myself and tragically forget the underbelly of the person criticizing—the place where they are vulnerable and might be hiding things, protected beneath their harsh words and a prickly exterior.

This is a place they may never let me see. It's the storage place for their hurts and disappointments. It holds the root cause of their skepticism and the anger that probably has very little to do with me. "For the mouth speaks what the heart is full of" (Matthew 12:34). And from the overflow of their hurt, they spewed.

Remember, behind every harsh critic is usually a brokenhearted person desperate for love.

If I forget the other person's vulnerability, I am tempted to start storing up my own hurt, skepticism, anger, and disappointments.

If I remember this underbelly, I have a much greater chance to keep it all in perspective. I can let my reaction be a good example to this other person just as our key verse,

> *Remember, behind every harsh critic is usually a brokenhearted person desperate for love.*

Luke 21:13–15, reminds us: "It will lead to an opportunity for you to witness. Therefore make up your minds not to prepare your defense ahead of time, for I will give you such words and a wisdom that none of your adversaries will be able to resist or contradict."

When criticism comes—and it will—I must make up my mind not to worry about defending myself. I can resist the urge to become prickly and use it as an opportunity to be a witness. A witness of the love, grace, and mercy of Jesus. Things I desperately need myself.

Dear Lord, thank You for this challenge to think about the other person's underbelly before I react to criticism. I know it's a simple step, but it's so hard to live out. Help me put this truth into practice and to walk in the wisdom You have already given me. In Jesus' Name, Amen.

85

I Had the Perfect Comeback

Only let us live up to what we have already attained.
—Philippians 3:16

*D*o you sometimes feel like you want to put your Christianity on a shelf and be as mean to someone as they were being to you?

Maybe not, because you are nice. And most of the time, I am too.

But recently, I had a moment where the mean girl inside of me wanted to be heard.

I was on a plane with two of my friends. We were talking in normal conversational tones when suddenly the couple in the next row up came unglued.

The man turned around and said, "Can you guys just QUIET DOWN already?"

It wasn't a gentle suggestion. It was a harsh command.

A little stunned, we simply replied, "Sure, we just . . ."

Before I could finish my sentence, his wife whipped her head around and snapped, "Your constant talking has given me a migraine. So just HUSH, okay?"

My heart raced. My face turned red. And I thought of the perfect comeback to say. I won't tell you what I wanted to say, but I can assure you it didn't involve being kind or gentle.

This is the exact point where I had to make a choice.

A choice of whom I wanted to partner with in this situation . . . God or Satan.

If I'd chosen the route of anger, a harsh comeback and retaliation, I would have basically stepped into Satan's camp and caused conflict escalation. If, however, I'd chosen the route of gentleness and grace, I would be partnering with God and would continue to make progress with my raw emotions. Like Philippians 3:16 reminds me, "Only let us live up to what we have already attained."

Why would I want to trade the peace of partnering with God for a few cheap moments of putting someone else in their place?

On my journey of improving my reactions, I have already attained more gentleness, more grace, more peace. Why would I want to trade all that for a few minutes of retaliating words? Words that will only leave me with a big ol' pile of regret.

Now I can't promise I've progressed to the point where my initial thoughts about this couple were nice. They weren't. But I chose to consider the reality that people who are that on edge must have a lot of stored-up misery. Their reaction probably had a lot less to do with me and a lot more to do with another situation in their lives.

My job wasn't to fix them or set them straight or prove how wrong they were acting.

My job in that moment was to keep everything in perspective. And simply give a gentle answer that could turn away their wrath.

While it felt hugely offensive when it was happening, it wasn't huge. This wasn't some sort of major injustice in my life. This was just a minor inconvenience. Why would I want to trade the peace of partnering with God for a few cheap moments of putting someone else in their place?

It's all about perspective.

Because in all honesty, if this was the worst thing that happened to me that day, it was still a pretty good day!

Dear Lord, You are so good and faithful. Thank You for helping me keep things in perspective so I can work on having better reactions that honor You. In Jesus' Name, Amen.

86

GOD, GIVE US SELF-CONTROL

As the rain and the snow
    come down from heaven,
and do not return to it
    without watering the earth
and making it bud and flourish,
    so that it yields seed for the sower and
        bread for the eater,
so is my word that goes out from my mouth:
    It will not return to me empty,
but will accomplish what I desire
    and achieve the purpose for which I sent it.

—ISAIAH 55:10–11

Have you ever been in a discussion with a loved one and suddenly your blood pressure skyrockets, your nerves fray, and the worst version of you begs to come out?

Not that this ehhhhhver happens to me of course.

Ahem.

Of course it happens to me. I live with other humans. But what I'm trying to better understand is this whole concept of self-control. So many times in the Bible we are told to display self-control: Proverbs 25:28, Galatians 5:23, 1 Peter 4:7, and many others.

But it's hard to display self-control when it feels like someone else does things out of our control and yanks our emotions into a bad place. So, here's one little tidbit I'm learning. When someone else's actions or statements threaten to pull me into a bad place, I have a choice. I do. It may feel like I don't have a choice. It may feel like I have to react according to my feelings, but I don't. I have a choice.

My choice is whether to give them the power to control my emotions.

When I react by yelling or flying off the handle or making a snappy comment back, I basically transfer my power to that other person. When I'm void of power, I'm void of self-control. So, it seems to me if I'm going to remain self-controlled, I have to keep my power.

The answer to keeping God's power with me and working in me to produce self-control is letting His Word get inside me.

Now, when I say, "my power," I don't mean something I conjure up myself. I am referring to God's power working in me. When I react according to God's Word, I feel that power. When I react contrary to God's Word, I feel powerless.

Isaiah 55:10–11 is such a good reminder of how we can tap into God's power no matter what situation we are facing:

> As the rain and the snow
> > come down from heaven,
> and do not return to it
> > without watering the earth

and making it bud and flourish,

so that it yields seed for the sower and bread for the eater,

so is my word that goes out from my mouth:

It will not return to me empty,

but will accomplish what I desire

and achieve the purpose for which I sent it. (emphasis mine)

Did you catch that? The answer to keeping God's power with me and working in me to produce self-control is letting His Word get inside me. His Word seeping into my mind and my heart will accomplish things—good things, powerful things—things that help me display self-control.

So, here's my new tactic. When I'm facing a situation where someone is aggravating me, I'm going to start quoting God's Word in the present tense. Take 1 Peter 5:6–8 for example: "Humble yourselves, therefore, under God's mighty hand, that he may lift you up in due time. Cast all your anxiety on him because he cares for you. Be alert and of sober mind. Your enemy the devil prowls around like a roaring lion looking for someone to devour."

And declare it like this, "In this moment, I'm choosing to be self-controlled and alert. Your actions are begging me to yell and lose control. But, I realize I have an Enemy and that Enemy is not you. The Devil is prowling and roaring and looking to devour me through my own lack of control right now. But I am God's girl. That's right. I am. So, I am going to humbly and quietly let God have His way in me right now. And when I do this, God will lift me and my frayed nerves up from this situation and fill me with a much better reaction than what I can give you right now. So, give me just a few minutes and then we'll calmly talk about this."

Girl, that's some power right there.

And that will make you shine with so much self-control your kids, friends, loved ones and coworkers won't know what to do with you.

That statement was just taken from one little set of verses found in 1 Peter that we'll dig into even more tomorrow. But can you imagine what might happen if we wrote out powerful responses using God's Word on cards and pulled them out every time we found ourselves in a situation? I love being God's girl.

Dear Lord, I am reminded that I am Your child. You made me. You know me. When I lack my own power to be self-controlled, help me turn to Your truth for good, calm responses. In Jesus' Name, Amen.

87

WHAT TO DO WITH TOUGH RELATIONSHIPS

Humble yourselves, therefore, under God's mighty
hand, that he may lift you up in due time.
—1 PETER 5:6

elationships are hard to navigate sometimes. If you're in the midst of trying to figure out a situation that's complicated, messy, and unpredictable, I imagine you're nodding your head in agreement right now.

Sometimes I try so hard to figure out just the right words to say and talk through a situation. While talking is good, sometimes the conversations start running in a circle, and there aren't any productive words left to say. When this happens, it can make a girl feel like giving up. But before I give up, I've learned to hush up.

The truth is, we have an Enemy, and it's not each other.

Spending time getting quiet can be the best remedy for tangled situations. Taking a step back from all the emotion, frustration, and exhaustion to sit quietly with Jesus will do more to untangle a mess than anything else I've ever found.

Here are five beautiful things that can happen in the quiet:

1. We can feel safe enough to humble ourselves. In the heat of a mess, the last thing I want to do is get humble. I want to get loud

and prove my point. I've learned I have to step out of the battle and humbly ask God to speak truth to my heart for things to start to make sense. Never have I had a relationship issue where I didn't contribute at least something to the problem. Usually, I can only see this something in the quiet.

1 Peter 5:6: "Humble yourselves, therefore, under God's mighty hand."

2. God will lift us up to a more rational place. When we are in the heat of a tangled relationship, crazy emotions can drag us down into a pit of hopelessness. The only way out of the pit is to make the choice to stop digging deeper and turn to God for a solution.

1 Peter 5:6: ". . . that he may lift you up in due time."

3. Anxiety gives way to progress. We can pour our anxious hearts out to Jesus who loves us right where we are, how we are. And because His love comes without judgment, we can feel safe enough to humbly admit we need Jesus to work on us. Trying to fix another person will only add to my anxiety. Letting Jesus work on me is where real progress can happen.

1 Peter 5:7: "Cast all your anxiety on him because he cares for you."

4. We see our real Enemy isn't the person with whom we're in conflict. The truth is, we have an Enemy, and it's not each other. Satan's influence on me *and* the person offending me is the real culprit. I can't realize this in the heat of the moment. But in the quiet, I become alert and can gain a strategy for acting and reacting in a more self-controlled manner.

1 Peter 5:8–9: "Be alert and of sober mind. Your enemy the devil prowls around like a roaring lion looking for someone to devour. Resist him, standing firm in the faith."

5. I can rest assured God will use this conflict for good—no matter how it turns out. **If I make the effort to handle this conflict well, I can be freed from the pressure to make everything turn out rosy. Because I can't control the other person, I must keep focusing on the good God is working out in me through this and leave the outcome with Him.**

1 Peter 5:10–11: "And the God of all grace, who called you to his eternal glory in Christ, after you have suffered a little while, will himself restore you and make you strong, firm, and steadfast. To him be the power for ever and ever. Amen."

In the end, this struggle can be used by God to make me stronger and more capable in my relationships. If I am humble enough to receive from Him in the quiet what He wants to teach me through this, I can rest assured with whatever the outcome is.

Dear Lord, help me stop trying to figure this situation out and just sit in the quiet with You for a while. Humble me. Take my anxiety and replace it with Your peace, wisdom, and security. I trust in You. In Jesus' Name, Amen.

88

You Don't Like Me

Do not be anxious about anything.
—Philippians 4:6

Have you ever been taunted by toxic thoughts? I have.

You are not liked.

Who are you to think you could do that?

Why did you say that? Everyone thinks you're annoying.

Your kids just illustrated every inadequacy you have as a mom.

You are invisible.

Why do we let such destructive words fall hard on our souls? Toxic thoughts are so dangerous because they leave no room for truth to flourish. And in the absence of truth, lies reign.

As Christian women, we need to focus on holding our thoughts to a higher standard. How dare these runaway thoughts be allowed to simply parade about as if they are true and manipulate us into feeling insecure, inadequate, and misunderstood! Oh, how much trouble we invite into our lives based on assumptions. But God's Word instructs us:

Do not be anxious about anything, but in every situation, by prayer and petition, with thanksgiving, present your requests to God. And the peace of God, which transcends all understanding, will guard your hearts and your minds in Christ Jesus. Finally, brothers and sisters, whatever is true, whatever is noble, whatever is right, whatever is pure, whatever is lovely, whatever is admirable—if anything is excellent or praiseworthy—think about such things. Whatever you have learned or received or heard from me, or seen in me—put it into practice. And the God of peace will be with you. (Philippians 4:6–9)

In the absence of truth, lies reign.

This is probably a passage you've read before. But, have you thought of applying it to your every thought—especially the toxic ones?

The mind feasts on what it focuses on. What consumes our thinking will be the making or breaking of our identity.

That's why we need to think on, ponder, and park our minds on constructive thoughts—not destructive thoughts. Thoughts that build up, not tear down. Thoughts that breathe life, not drain the life from us. Thoughts that lead to goodness, not anxiety.

So, here are three questions we'd do well to ask ourselves when thoughts are dragging us down.

1. Did someone actually say this or am I assuming they are thinking it? If they actually said it, deal with it then. If I'm assuming it, that's unfair to them and unnecessarily damaging to me. Instead of staying anxious, I need to seek truth by seeking God and asking Him for peace.

"Do not be anxious about anything, but in every situation, by prayer and petition, with thanksgiving, present your requests to God" (Philippians 4:6).

2. Have I been actively engaging with truth lately? The more we

read God's truths and let truth fill our mind, the less time we'll spend contemplating untruths.

Thinking runaway, worrisome thoughts invites anxiety. Thinking thoughts of truth wraps my mind in peace and helps me rise above my circumstances.

"And the peace of God, which transcends all understanding, will guard your hearts and your minds in Christ Jesus" (Philippians 4:7).

3. Are certain situations or friendships feeding my insecurities? If so, maybe I need to take a break from these for a season.

I need to seek friendships that are characterized by truth, honor, and love.

"Finally, brothers and sisters, whatever is true, whatever is noble, whatever is right, whatever is pure, whatever is lovely, whatever is admirable—if anything is excellent or praiseworthy—think about such things" (Philippians 4:8).

I know this is tough stuff. I know these issues can be more complicated than three simple questions. But it's a good place to start holding our thoughts accountable.

After all, how a woman thinks is often how she lives. May we think upon and live out truth—and only truth—today.

Dear Lord, reveal to me untruths throughout my day that can so easily distract and discourage me. Help me see You and Your truth in all I do. In Jesus' Name, Amen.

89

COMPARISONS STINK

*If anyone thinks they are something when they are not,
they deceive themselves. Each one should test their
own actions. Then they can take pride in themselves
alone, without comparing themselves to someone
else, for each one should carry their own load.*

—GALATIANS 6:3–5

Comparisons stink. They do.

Just when I think I've gotten to a good place in some area of my life, along comes someone or something that seems better in comparison. And my confidence shrinks back, takes the hand of doubt, and starts ransacking the peace right out of my heart and mind.

I know deep down that God *can* and *will* use everything for good in my life, even my areas of vulnerability. But honest to goodness, it's hard on a girl's heart.

Not too long ago, I was in a situation where something I'm very self-conscious about was magnified when compared to others' near-perfection. I was at the beach with several friends who have dancer's legs. And by dancer, I mean like twenty-year-old, ballerina-perfection legs.

I guess you could say I have dancer legs too if you are referring to the dancing hippo from the children's movie *Madagascar*.

Apparently, long, lean legs just aren't in my genetic makeup, even though I can eat healthy and exercise every bit as much as my ballerina-like friends.

So there I was on the beach. Comparing my vulnerable place to their perceived strength.

And in the private space of my most inner thoughts, I cried. I found myself feeling defeated and convinced that this area will always be a struggle for me.

Oh, I can make progress, for sure. Heaven knows, I do work on it. And most days, I see how God is using this all for good. But when comparison sneaks in, it can be hard. Worse than hard. It can quite simply make me forget all the strengths I do have.

And when I forget, my heart shifts. I stop being thankful and instead become consumed by that thing I don't have.

Satan will always try to point out what's "wrong" to block out all that is right. And his whispers sound pretty convincing sometimes.

Satan will always try to point out what's "wrong" to block out all that is right.

But that's a dangerous place to park your mind.

In moments like these I find myself needing to soak in the truths of Galatians 6:3–5, "If anyone thinks they are something when they are not, they deceive themselves. Each one should test their own actions. Then they can take pride in themselves alone, without comparing themselves to someone else, for each one should carry their own load."

As I thought more about that day on the beach, I realized I wasn't prayed up. Knowing I might have some comparison issues, I should have asked God to help keep my focus on Him. Instead, I just found myself wallowing—and wallowing isn't of the Lord. Amen? Amen!

I share this because you need to know that we all struggle. I'm on a journey of learning. Just like you.

And I desperately need God's truth to bump into my weaknesses every single day. Only then can I get out of the shadow of doubt and into the life-giving reality of who God has made me to be. And see it as good. Not perfect. Not even close. But good. And good is good.

Dear Lord, forgive me for all the times I've compared myself to others. I know You have hand-picked all my qualities. Help me see these things as beautiful reminders of Your great love in creating me as Your daughter. In Jesus' Name, Amen.

90

HER SUCCESS DOESN'T THREATEN MINE

These were his instructions to them: "The harvest is great,
but the workers are few. So pray to the Lord who is in charge
of the harvest; ask him to send more workers into his fields."
—LUKE 10:2 NLT

*H*ave you ever wondered if there's any need for you and the dreams tucked in your heart, when there are already so many successful people out there in the world?

I totally understand.

Several years ago, I remember pouring out all the best words I had through a pixelated letters-turned-pages-turned-book proposal. I tucked my heart and dreams into a purple Office Max binder and hoped for the best.

That summer, I gave my proposal to several acquisitions editors. For months after sending out my proposal, I would dream about the day some publishing house would say yes.

I can't tell you the number of afternoons I'd stand at my mailbox, holding my breath, praying there would be good news inside. When the rejection letters started coming, I tried to keep up the hope that surely there would be one positive answer. I just needed one publisher to say yes.

Soon, I'd received a "no" answer from all but one. And when I got that final rejection, I felt so foolish for thinking I could actually write a book. My dream was nothing but a sham. I had no writing skills. And I must have heard God all wrong.

All tides rise when we see a sister making this world a better place with her gifts.

At the same time, I had other writer friends who were getting different letters from the publishers.

Amazing letters.

Dreams-come-true letters.

Letters that turned into book contracts.

In my better moments, I did the right thing and authentically celebrated with them. But then there were other moments. Hard moments.

Moments where I felt my friends' lives were rushing past me in a flurry of met goals, new opportunities, and affirmations of their callings from God. It seemed the world was passing me by. And in those moments I said on the outside, "Good for them."

But on the inside, I just kept thinking, *Ouch . . . that means less and less opportunity for me.* The raw essence of honest hurting rarely produces pretty thoughts.

I wrestled and I processed.

And I decided to get still. Refusing to believe I'd been left out and left behind. And starving my scarcity thinking.

Those times of being still are good and necessary when your thinking needs to be swept all into one pile. Then it's much easier to identify treasures to keep, from the trash that should be tossed.

Then I could see new and life-giving realities. Her success does not threaten yours, nor mine. When she does well, we all do well. All tides rise when we see a sister making this world a better place with her gifts.

When I finally started believing this, my stillness turned into readiness. And that was twenty-one published books ago.

This is what Jesus reminds us: "The harvest is great, but the workers are few. So pray to the Lord who is in charge of the harvest; ask him to send more workers into his fields" (Luke 10:2 NLT).

And this is where we have a choice to make today.

We can look out and see the unlimited, abundant opportunities God has placed before us. To create. To write. To serve. To sing. To be and become.

Or we can stare at another person's opportunity and get entangled in the Enemy's lie that everything is scarce. Scarce opportunities. Scarce supply. Scarce possibilities. And we start seeing another person's creations as a threat to our own opportunities.

Oh, sweet sister, there is an abundant need in this world for your contributions to the Kingdom . . . your thoughts and words and artistic expressions . . . your exact brand of beautiful.

Know it. Believe it. Live it.

Lord, today, I'm asking You to bless the women around me doing what I long to do. Stir even more hearts with a deep passion to make You known. And continue to settle my heart with the truth that this world really does need my exact brand of beautiful. In Jesus' Name, Amen.

91

I Want What She Has

A heart at peace gives life to the body,
but envy rots the bones.
—Proverbs 14:30

Chances are, if you're like me, you've struggled with these areas I've been talking about—comparison and envy.

My house looks great until a friend redecorates. Her clever color combination and crafty restoration abilities have created rooms that look as though they've stepped straight from a magazine. Suddenly my home feels outdated and plain.

My kids always seemed great until I was around someone else's who excelled in areas my kids struggled in. I would see her kids quietly reading books that were well advanced for their age and loving every minute of it. I compared that to mine who would have rather had their right arms cut off than read books that were barely grade level all the while asking me when they could go do something else more exciting. Suddenly I was judging myself for not making reading more of a priority when they were younger and felt like a subpar mom.

No, it doesn't take long for all that I'm blessed with to pale in the face of comparison. I'm blinded from seeing what I do have in the face of what I don't have. My heart is drawn into a place of ungratefulness and assumption. As I assume everything is great for those who possess what I don't, I become less and less thankful for what's mine. I forget the warning tucked in Proverbs 14:30, "A heart at peace gives life to the body, but envy rots the bones."

And here's the real kicker . . . things for the person I'm comparing myself to are almost never what they seem. Everybody has not-so-great sides to their lives. Whenever I get an idyllic view of someone else's life, I will often say out loud, "I am not equipped to handle what they have, both good and bad."

God has taught me a lot about how to nip a comparison in the bud so it doesn't develop into full-blown envy and jealously.

The statement, "I am not equipped to handle what they have, both good and bad," has been one of the greatest realizations God has given me. Every situation has both good and bad. When I want someone else's good, I must realize that I'm also asking for the bad that comes along with it. It's always a package deal. And usually if I'll just give something enough time to unfold, I can often be found thanking God that I didn't get someone else's package.

I am not equipped to handle what they have, both good and bad.

One of the first times I came to understand this truth was in middle school when I met a beautiful girl at the Children's Theater in my town. We were both budding child actors cast in a Christmas play. During rehearsals I can remember seeing her long dancer's legs move in ways my stubby limbs never could. Her legs were muscular and lean and graceful. Mine couldn't be described with any of those adjectives.

One day there was an unusual pain in her left leg. And then a doctor's appointment turned into a battery of tests that turned into a hospital stay that turned into a diagnosis. Cancer. A surgery to remove a tumor turned into an amputation turned into a complete life change. Her world became filled with words no child should ever have to know: chemotherapy, prosthetics, hair loss, and walking canes.

As a young girl I was stunned by the whole thing. Especially because I clearly remember night after night after watching her glide across stage, I would ask God for legs exactly like hers.

Not equipped to handle what they have, both good and bad.

I don't want to paint the picture that every good thing someone else has will end with a tragedy. That's not the case. Sometimes others' good things are simply fantastic. But they are fantastic for them— not me.

Dear Lord, thank You for only entrusting me with what
I have and who I am. In Jesus' Name, Amen.

92

But, Lord, I Can't DO That!

Moses said to the LORD, "Pardon your servant, Lord. I have never been eloquent, neither in the past nor since you have spoken to your servant. I am slow of speech and tongue."

—EXODUS 4:10

Insecurities. We all have them.

These qualities about ourselves that make us lack confidence or assurance can be a positive call to action to make healthy changes in our lives.

But insecurities can also hold us back from stepping into the assignments God calls us to.

That's exactly what happened in the place where we find Moses in our key verse today.

Moses knew with absolute certainty what God was calling Him to do. God had confirmed it by speaking to him audibly through a burning bush telling him, "to bring my people the Israelites out of Egypt" (Exodus 3:10).

And Moses knew exactly what to say, what God planned to do, that God would be with him, and that God would provide for them with plunder from the Egyptians.

So, what could possibly hold him back when things seemed so very clear?

It was the same thing that might be holding you and me back at times.

Moses doubted God had created him for the calling God gave him.

In Exodus 4:10 Moses says to the Lord, "Pardon your servant, Lord. I have never been eloquent, neither in the past nor since you have spoken to your servant. I am slow of speech and tongue."

The exact way God made you is in keeping with how He will use you.

The Lord comes back with very strong words to Moses, "Who gave human beings their mouths? . . . Now go; I will help you speak and will teach you what to say" (vv. 11–12).

When we doubt we have what it takes for us to do what God calls us to do, we are doubting His creative abilities. He knew from the beginning of time what He would call you to do and therefore how you would need to be formed. God does everything with purpose and precision.

The exact way He made you is in keeping with how He will use you.

Trust this. Embrace this. Even if you don't know all the details of your calling quite yet, thank God for making you perfectly equipped for your assignments ahead.

And when insecurities start to make you doubt, flip it around and say, "God, I may doubt myself. But I will not doubt You. So, I will let Your perfection override my feelings of imperfection and do what You instruct me."

Heavenly Father, I confess that all too often I doubt I have what it takes to do the things You have called me to do. Remind me I have been perfectly equipped for the assignments You have given me. Help me not to doubt or compare. In Jesus' Name, Amen.

93

FEELING GUILTY?

I praise you because I am fearfully and
wonderfully made;
your works are wonderful,
I know that full well.

—PSALM 139:14

*J*gathered the restaurant bags, sighed, and crammed them into the overstuffed trash can. A friend had sent me a recipe that day which involved peeling and chopping and simmering. I imagined her trash can full of fresh veggie peelings and other things that proved her kitchen produced way more homemade goodness than mine.

And a little thread of guilt wrapped around my heart.

Sometimes I feel more guilty for what I'm not than thankful for what I am.

But there was sweet grace waiting for me in a yogurt shop that night. My oldest daughter, Hope, had asked if I would come and speak to a little Bible study she was helping organize. "Mom, I think there are going to be a lot of people who show up."

So, instead of cooking that night, I ordered out. Again. And then I drove to the yogurt shop with the girl whose heart was full of excitement and expectation.

People were everywhere. Young people. Invited people. And parents.

Nearly two hundred people packed inside the yogurt shop and over-flowed onto the sidewalk outside. Hope smiled.

Sometimes I feel more guilty for what I'm not than thankful for what I am.

I took the microphone and spoke from my heart. I told my story. I taught truth. I invited the people to let Jesus be the Lord of their hearts.

And many who had never done so said yes to God that night. A teen girl who'd tried to commit suicide the year before stood to accept Jesus. A young man with tears in his eyes stood to accept Jesus. A mom and a dad stood to accept Jesus. Along with many others.

In the yogurt shop.

With a woman whose trash can was filled with takeout bags.

A woman who isn't the greatest cook. But a woman who wants to learn to be more thankful for what I am than guilty for what I'm not. A woman who wants the truth of Psalm 139:14 to be the declaration of my soul: "I praise you because I am fearfully and wonderfully made; your works are wonderful, I know that full well."

Maybe you are the friend with the veggie peelings in the trash can and steaming homemade goodness on the table.

Celebrate that.

Or maybe you are like me. And your gifts are less tasty.

Celebrate that.

And cut the threads of guilt with the edge of grace.

Dear Lord, You made me in Your image and that is something I seem to forget daily. Please help me remember to celebrate and live in who You made me to be and not in what I wish I were. In Jesus' Name, Amen.

94

EVEN WHEN I FALL SHORT

Though the righteous fall seven times, they
rise again,
but the wicked stumble when calamity
strikes.

—PROVERBS 24:16

*R*ewarding. That's what this particular day was supposed to be, my shining-star day at my kids' school. Finally, I was going to get the "Really Good Mommy Award."

This is not an official award on a frame-worthy piece of fine linen paper. It's just a feeling—that feeling of getting a thumbs-up and acceptance nod that you are in fact doing an okay job as a mom.

I had volunteered to make one hundred individually wrapped homemade brownies. And I was going to be completely fancy and use the turtle brownie mix that comes in a box. That's as close to home-made as I get.

After baking all those brownies and allowing them to cool, I cut and lifted each one into the safety of its own little baggie and recruited my daughters to help me finish up. We bagged up brownies ninety-five, ninety-six, ninety-seven, and then a disaster of epic proportions occurred.

Nuts.

These turtle brownies had nuts in them. Lots of nuts. And there I was standing over individually wrapped brownie number ninety-seven listening to my daughter's reminder that our school was, in fact, a peanut-free school.

My arms started flailing about as if to gather the pieces of my scattered brain and tuck everything back into place. I sent the kids out of the room and ate brownies ninety-eight, ninety-nine, and one hundred.

No shining star. No Really Good Mommy Award. No happy, proud kids elated with their mom's efforts.

When circumstances shift and we feel like we fall short, we should ask, How can I see Jesus even in this?

I spent the rest of the day trying to process this great brownie failure. I saw it as a debacle that defined my motherhood journey. Grand visions that led to big messes that led to unmet expectations that heaped more and more guilt on my already slightly fragile motherhood psyche.

And that's exactly where Satan would have loved for me to stay. That's his daily goal, actually. If Satan can use our everyday experiences, both big and small, to cripple our true identities, then he renders God's people totally ineffective for the Kingdom of Christ.

These were brownies for a school bake sale. And these brownies had somehow knocked me to the ground. I didn't want to smile. I didn't want to be kind. I didn't want to be a disciple for Christ that day. Ever been there?

Satan wants us to entertain a very dangerous thought: *Why doesn't*

Jesus work for me? This is never the right question. Instead, when circumstances shift and we feel like we fall short, we should ask, *How can I see Jesus even in this?*

The only way I can ask myself this question is when I pull back from whatever situation I'm facing and separate my circumstance from my identity.

Now let's state what is true. Despite my feelings, my identity stayed the same. I am a loving mom. I am a giving person. I am a woman who takes her responsibilities seriously. I am a daughter of the King.

All of this is true despite my failures. So, though I had a whole mess of extra brownies with nuts laying around and the school didn't have any brownies for the bake sale that day, this mishap didn't define me. The only thing it meant was that I needed to read the bake sale instruction sheet a little closer next time.

That's it. It's simply a call to action not a call to condemnation. And did you notice the response of the righteous man in Proverbs 24:16? Though he fell time and again, he kept getting up. May we do the very same thing.

Dear Lord, help me separate my circumstances from my identity. Help me only determine my worth by Your truth and not my performance in any situation. Thank You for looking at me not as I am, but how Jesus has enabled me to be. In Jesus' Name, Amen.

95

THE FRIENDSHIP CHALLENGE

Two are better than one,
    because they have a good return for their
      labor:
If either of them falls down,
    one can help the other up.
But pity anyone who falls
    and has no one to help them up.
Also, if two lie down together, they will keep
    warm.
    But how can one keep warm alone?
      —ECCLESIASTES 4:9–11

*W*hat makes a woman tender also reveals her vulnerabilities.
    What makes a woman transparent also exposes her wounds.
What makes a woman authentic also uncovers her insecurities.

And there aren't many women who enjoy being revealed, exposed, and uncovered. But establishing real intimacy with another person requires pushing past the resistance—past the fear.

Friendship is risky.

To be known is to risk being hurt. But friendship can be beautiful, and worth the risk.

We can look to the Bible for examples of monumental friendships.

In 1 Samuel 18 we learn about the special friendship between David and Jonathan, an example of a true bond. When Jonathan's father, King Saul, threatened David with death, Jonathan risked his position in his father's household and warned his friend.

Jonathan and David's friendship lasted their lifetime, and because of Jonathan's loyalty to David, the Lord blessed them both. David eventually became king, but by then Jonathan had died. David inquired, "Is there anyone still left of the house of Saul to whom I can show kindness for Jonathan's sake?" (2 Samuel 9:1).

Don't miss this beauty: it was customary for the present king to put to death any of the former king's family. However, because of his and Jonathan's strong friendship, King David tenderly provided for Jonathan's son. "I will restore to you all the land that belonged to your grandfather Saul, and you will always eat at my table" (v. 7). "So Mephibosheth ate at David's table like one of the king's sons" (v. 11).

Awesome. Inspiring. Friendship.

Yes, friendship is beautiful. The Lord gave it to us. He knew we would need each other to get through this life. He even tells us in Ecclesiastes 4:9 that "two are better than one."

Think about a friend you can make an investment in.

Not the friend with whom you feel most comfortable. But rather one who might benefit from seeing a little more of your tenderness, transparency, and authenticity. Someone who might be worth a risk.

Someone in your sphere of influence is desperate to know someone else understands.

Might we take three steps and give

The Lord knew we would need each other to get through this life.

ourselves a friendship challenge? Here are three things you can do to invest in a friend:

1. Have a conversation with her in which you honestly admit one of your vulnerabilities. Chances are she'll reveal something to you as well. Then really commit to pray for her. Maybe wear a watch or bracelet and every time you're distracted by it, use this as a prompt to carry her burden in your prayers.

2. Buy or make this friend a gift. Just because. It doesn't have to cost much. But make an investment of time to think of something that would personally delight her.

3. Write your friend a note to attach to the gift. In the letter, tell her at least three things you admire about her and some way she's made a difference in your life.

Then deliver this little "just because" gift and note to your friend. This friend who sometimes feels a little vulnerable. Wounded. Exposed in some way.

Your honesty and thoughtfulness will be such a sweet investment.

For her.

For you.

For your friendship.

Are you up for taking the friendship challenge?

Dear Lord, thank You for the friendships and beautiful blessings You have placed in my life. Help me to see this challenge as a sweet reminder to show Your love to those around me. In Jesus' Name, Amen.

96

THE SCRIBBLED TRUTH
THAT CHANGED MY LIFE

Peter said, "Silver or gold I do not have,
but what I do have I give you."
—ACTS 3:6

When my baby sister died tragically and unexpectedly, my entire world flipped upside-down. It was a very dark season of my life. What I once knew to be true suddenly became questionable.

Is God good? If so, why this? And if I never know why, how can I ever trust God again?

Hard questions. Honest questions. Questions that haunted me.

Until one day, I got a note from a friend. A girl I not-so-affectionately called my "Bible friend." She honestly got on my nerves with all her Bible verse quoting. I wasn't on good terms with God at that point in my life. I didn't want to believe God even existed. And I certainly wasn't reading the Bible.

I made all of this very known to my Bible friend. But in her gentle, sweet, kind way . . . she kept slipping me notes of truth with gently woven verses tucked within. And one day, one verse cracked the dam of my soul. Truth slipped in and split my hard-hearted views of life open, just enough for God to make Himself known to me.

I held that simple note with one Bible verse scribbled on the front as the tears of honest need streamed down my cheeks. My stiff knees bent. And a whispered, *"Yes, God,"* changed the course of my life.[1] (If you have never whispered *yes* to God, you can find a salvation prayer on page 315.)

I will never doubt the power of one woman reaching into the life of another woman with some written whispers of love.

My Bible friend had reached me. And because of her, I'm determined to use my words as a gift to others who may be in hard places . . . like a friend of mine who recently told me she is struggling with feeling like she has no real purpose.

Life rushes at her each day with overwhelming demands. Everything feels hard, with very little reprieve.

If ever there were a drowning with no water involved, this is where my friend is. Maybe you have a hurting friend, too.

So I sat down to write my friend a card and send her a little gift. I desperately wanted to love her through my words. My heart was full of care, compassion, and a strong desire to encourage, but I struggled to translate all I felt on paper.

As I prayed about it, the word *loved* kept coming to mind.

Remind her she is loved. Remind her how much you respect her. Remind her that she is a woman who has so much to offer. Remind her she is valuable and she is enough.

In Acts 3, Peter and John encountered a crippled man at the temple gate called Beautiful. They stopped. They noticed. They decided to touch. Riches weren't available to them but the ability to value was.

As Acts 3:6–7 says, "'Silver or gold I do not have, but what I do have I give you. In the name of Jesus Christ of Nazareth, walk.' Taking him by the right hand, he helped him up."

Peter and John didn't have silver, but they had a hand to offer and value to give. The man in need was worth touching. The hurting one in need was a man who needed someone to see him as a man. The man in need had so much to offer. After he got up, he went into the temple courts, praising God and stirring up wonder and amazement about God.

I want my friend to remember that she, too, has praise left inside her for our God. She, too, can get up. She, too, can stir up amazement and wonder about our God.

Yes, she is loved and God has a good plan for her. I want to help her see that, just like my Bible friend did for me all those years ago.

I will never doubt the power of one woman reaching into the life of another woman with some written whispers of love.

Dear Lord, I'm so thankful for the relationships You've placed in my life. Would You help me discern what encouraging words my friend needs to hear today? I want to show her Your love. In Jesus' Name, Amen.

97

GETTING PAST MY PAST

Praise be to the God and Father of our Lord Jesus
Christ, the Father of compassion and the God of
all comfort, who comforts us in all our troubles,
so that we can comfort those in any trouble with
the comfort we ourselves receive from God.

—2 CORINTHIANS 1:3–4

Is there something from your past that haunts you and constantly interrupts your thoughts?

For many years, that something in my life was my abortion. I walked around in a zombielike state in the months following that decision with a growing hatred for myself at the root of my pain and confusion.

Up until that point, the things that brought hurt into my life were caused by others. But the abortion was a choice I made myself. It seemed like the only answer at the time. The abortion clinic workers assured me that they could take care of this "problem" quickly and easily, so I would never have to think about it again. What a lie.

I kept my secret buried deep within my heart. I was so ashamed, so horrified, so convinced that if anyone ever found out I'd had an abortion, I'd be rejected by all my church friends and deemed a woman unfit to serve God.

My complete healing began when I was finally able to turn my thoughts past my own healing to helping others in the same situation. It was terrifying to think about sharing my story with another person. But then I heard of a young girl our family knew who was in a crisis pregnancy situation. She was planning to have an abortion.

God truly can take even our worst mistakes and somehow bring good from them.

I was faced with a fierce tug of war in my spirit. I knew if she heard my story, she might make a different choice. *But what would she think of me? What would others think if they found out?* I knew God wanted me to talk to her. So would I trust Him, or would I retreat back into my shame?

With shaking hands, I approached Sydney, intent on extending God's comfort and compassion. Maybe I could just share a few Bible verses and offer to help her without making myself vulnerable.

But during our time together, it became clear she needed to hear my story. With a cracking voice and tear-filled eyes, I decided to care more about her situation than keeping my secret hidden. I told her the truth of what I'd experienced and prayed she'd make a different choice than I had.

A year after that first meeting, I sat across from Sydney once again. She choked out a whispered, "Thank you," as she turned and kissed the chubby-cheeked boy in the baby carrier beside her. As soon as she spoke those two life-defining words, tears fell from both of our eyes.

Hers were tears of relief.

Mine were tears of redemption.

Both were wrapped in the hope that God truly can take even our worst mistakes and somehow bring good from them.

God has brought me so far since that first meeting with Sydney. Now I travel to crisis pregnancy events and tell my story in hopes of encouraging people to support their local centers. I also share my story from pulpits all across America, trusting that the many women in the audience will see it is possible to be healed and restored from the tragic mistakes from our past.

But I can't reach everyone. There are women in your sphere of influence who need to hear *your* story.

I realize an abortion may not be the pain you're dealing with, but I also know few of us have escaped very deep hurts.

Will you go? Will you share? Will you allow God to comfort you and then take that comfort to others? This step could help you start your own healing process.

I think you'll find that you are the one who winds up doubly blessed as you walk out the truth of 2 Corinthians 1:3–4: "Praise be to the God and Father of our Lord Jesus Christ, the Father of compassion and the God of all comfort, who comforts us in all our troubles, so that we can comfort those in any trouble with the comfort we ourselves receive from God."

Dear Lord, only You can heal my deepest hurts and use the bad in my life for good. I need You more and more each day. Please continue to work in my life and use me as a light to help those You have entrusted to me. In Jesus' Name, Amen.

98

PUSHING PAST AWKWARD

Am I now trying to win the approval of human beings,
or of God? Or am I trying to please people? If I were still
trying to please people, I would not be a servant of Christ.
—GALATIANS 1:10

My fancy shoes tentatively stepped onto the red carpet. My consignment-store dress snagged on one of my heels as I took my first step. My face flushed. Not for the first little misstep in front of such a huge crowd but because of the sudden realization of just how disappointed the crowd was. I knew it. They knew it. And it was all so incredibly awkward.

I'd been invited to an awards night for musicians. I was one of just a couple of authors there for one book category. But the main focus of the night was the artistic talent of musicians. My art of stringing words together felt insignificant. Since my words had no beat, they seemed to have no place in the memory of those lining this red carpet.

They had cheered when the vehicle I was riding in pulled up. But as I stepped out, their whoops and hollers quieted. I was a sad disappointment, an unfamiliar face among bright musical stars.

I busied myself fidgeting with my purse and my dress and my cell phone. Awkward does this to us. It makes us fidget. In the midst of trying to comfort what feels so uncomfortable, we just feed the monster. Awkward gorges himself full in those insecure moments.

Appointments and disappointments walk hand in hand.

I'm not a musician. Just as a nonmusician girl feels out of place at a musicians' awards event, so will a Jesus girl feel out of place in a people-pleasing world.

You will sometimes feel exposed. Fidgety. Out of place. Insecure. And oh-so-incredibly awkward. These feelings aren't a sign that it's time to turn back. Or to give in to that people-pleasing desire beating against your fragile resolve. It's time to say to yourself, *I will not let the awkward disappointment of others keep me from my appointments with God.*

Do you know what I wanted to do that night on the red carpet? I wanted to get back in that vehicle, go back to the ease of my quiet hotel room, rip off that stupid, fancy dress, and crawl into bed, and pull the covers over my head. I did not want to keep walking that red carpet toward the awards ceremony I was supposed to attend. I did not want to push past that awkward disappointment of the crowd.

But if I was ever going to get where I was supposed to be that night, I was going to have to keep walking forward despite feeling awkward, despite the disappointment of others. And you know what happened once I got inside that awards ceremony? An appointment from God I wouldn't have ever experienced if I'd turned back.

Once inside I found a bathroom. Partly because I wanted to make sure my dress hadn't ripped in embarrassing places when my heel got caught. And partly because when you feel terribly awkward and out of place, bathroom stalls are glorious places to regroup.

When I walked in, there was a girl staring at herself in the mirror. I'm not especially inclined to make small talk, so I walked past her and into a stall. When I came out, she was still there. Still staring.

"You okay?" I asked.

"Not really." At first it was just those two words. But then more. And I realized her heart had been knocked around a bit out on that red carpet too. She was an amazingly talented musician. But her body size had been the topic of one too many hard conversations.

I guess because she didn't know me, she felt like she could open up to me. I wasn't in her music world, but I do personally know the pain of weight struggles. I know how thoughtless comments can cut deeply into a heart. And I know what it feels like to step on that scale and feel like a failure.

We talked. We shared. We laughed. And together we gained just a bit more courage. It was an appointment I wouldn't have experienced if I'd allowed disappointment to scare me away.

Appointments and disappointments walk hand in hand. I had to get past the disappointment of the crowd to receive this appointment from God.

Galatians 1:10 reminds us of why this is so important: "Am I now trying to win the approval of human beings, or of God? Or am I trying to please people? If I were still trying to please people, I would not be a servant of Christ." If we want to be the kind of people God can use anywhere at any time, we must get good at saying no to that resistance inside called awkwardness.

How do we learn to do this? We might think we just need to become more confident. But it goes deeper than that. It's not a matter of gaining more confidence. It's a matter of being more certain of our convictions. Confidence is being certain of our abilities. Conviction is being certain of God's instructions.

I'm not talking about the way we sometimes use the word *conviction* as a verb: *I'm convicted to wear longer shorts* or *I'm convicted to have more consistent quiet times*. The kind of conviction I'm referring to is a noun—a firm, foundational belief.

With a deep conviction that God's instruction can be trusted, we can learn to graciously push past awkward.

Dear Lord, please grant me the conviction I need to push past awkward. I don't want to miss any of the appointments You have for me. In Jesus' Name, Amen.

99

LIFE-SAVING TRUTH

If your law had not been my delight,
> I would have perished in my affliction.
I will never forget your precepts,
> for by them you have preserved my life.

—PSALM 119:92–93

I stood on the edge of the pool. I looked over at my sister who was maybe four or five at the time. She was splashing on the steps of the shallow end.

I'm done with the shallow end, I thought. *I'm nine years old. I'm very grown and old enough to jump into the deep end.*

I jumped. The cold water enveloped me. I let my body fall all the way until my toes touched the bottom, and I pushed myself back above water. It was exhilarating.

Each hot day when we showed up at the pool, we walked to our respective places. Me to the edge of the deep end with an ever-growing, brave heart. My sister to the stairs in the shallow end. But as the summer went on, I wondered, *Could I? Should I? Bring her out here to the deep?*

One day it occurred to me I could let her get on my back and half walk, half bounce down that slope between the shallow and the deep. I could go slowly. And if that next step deeper freaked her out, I could simply back up to where she felt comfortable.

I swam to the shallow end and unveiled my plan as if I were giving my sister the greatest gift one human could bestow on another.

Surprisingly, she was hesitant. It took great convincing on my part and lots of promises not to go any farther than where she felt safe.

Finally, she got on my back and wrapped her arms around my shoulders. I walked slowly to the slope. One baby step down. Two steps. Three.

At the third step, I slipped.

We both went under very suddenly. My sister's hands slipped from my shoulders to my throat. It was as if she believed the only way she could be saved was to hold my throat with an increasingly intense amount of strength. Her grip tightened to the point where even when I finally pushed up above the surface, no air could get in. My mind got foggy very quickly, and suddenly I couldn't figure out which way to go to find safety. I became less and less sure of most things around me, but absolutely sure about one thing. I was drowning.

Here's the craziest part of the story. I can't remember how we were saved. I know we were. My sister and I are both alive today. But I can't remember the rest of the story.

Maybe it's because I'm supposed to have the richest memories of that feeling of panic. And the realization that panic never helps save anyone.

You know where I see this drowning without water and a subsequent panicked response most often? A woman's insecurities.

I guarantee you've felt the choking effects of insecurity even if you don't call it that.

You're not as talented or smart or experienced as she is.

Protect yourself and your dignity. Don't dare try this new venture.

If only you were as organized or intentional or creative as they are, then maybe you could accomplish this. But the reality is, you're not.

You know this is never going to work, right?

How do I know you feel these things? Because I've experienced them myself.

Just like in that pool all those years ago, I can go from standing securely with my head above water to slipping down a slope with seemingly nothing to grab hold of. Then the insecurity, always kind of present on my shoulder, slips into a death grip around my throat.

My insecurities grip to the point where nothing life giving can get in. I forget truth. I don't even want to go to church. My mind gets foggy very quickly, and suddenly I can't figure out which way to go to find safety.

I'm drowning.

That's the thing about insecurity. When it grips us, the very thing we need most—truth—is the very thing we have a hard time grasping. I can be close to truth but still be drowning with my insecurities. I can have truth sitting on my nightstand. I can have it preached to me on Sundays. But grasping it and standing on it and letting it shift my thinking away from panic—that's something that requires truth to be more than just close.

That requires truth to be inside me, guiding me, rewiring my thinking, and whispering, "Safety is right here. Insecurity will stop choking you when you remove its grip. Insecurity only has power over you when you allow it control over your thoughts."

And as we delight in the truth of

The minute we receive Jesus to be the Lord of our lives, our limited potential can turn into exponential growth.

God's Word and live out the truth of God's Word, it truly becomes a lifeline to our souls. Something we see beautifully spelled out in our key verse: "If your law had not been my delight, I would have perished in my affliction. I will never forget your precepts, for by them you have preserved my life" (Psalm 119:92–93).

Indeed, we are limited in and of ourselves. But the minute we receive Jesus to be the Lord of our lives, our limited potential can turn into exponential growth. He is alive in us. He gives us freedom from our dead lives and the power to walk in a new life—a resurrected life.

I want to weave myself into your story. I'm standing in the shallow end. I'm holding tightly on to an immovable bar of truth with one hand—and with the other, I'm reaching toward you.

Grab hold. Come back from the sinking place. And from the deepest place of your soul, catch your breath.

Dear Lord, my insecurities are small things compared to Your truth. But they feel so big and powerful when they have a grip on me! Please help me grasp Your truth and let it change me. In Jesus' Name, Amen.

100

CALLED TO FREEDOM

*He who began a good work in you will carry it on
to completion until the day of Christ Jesus.*
—PHILIPPIANS 1:6

*L*abels are awful. They imprison us in categories that are hard to
escape. Maybe you are familiar with labels too ...

I am a wreck.

I am a people pleaser.

I am unglued.

I am an insecure mess.

And the list goes on.

Take my struggle with organization. Every day for months, I
walked in and out of my messy closet thinking, *Uggghhhh! Why am I so
disorganized? Why can't I have a closet like so-and-so? I don't think she ever
struggles with keeping things tidy. I'm just a mess.*

I labeled myself as a mess and then resigned myself to forever
being a mess.

Some prisons don't require bars to keep people locked inside. All
it takes is their perception that they belong there. A soul who believes
she can't leave ... doesn't.

I found my way out in an unexpected place.

I don't often visit museums. However, I'd read some fascinating facts about the *David* by Michelangelo and made it my mission to go and see the original at the Accademia Gallery in Florence, Italy.

Sources say the artist never left his *David*. For more than two years he worked on and slept beside the six-ton slab of marble whose subject called to him from inside the unchiseled places. When at last the seventeen-foot *David* emerged, Michelangelo is reported to have said, "I saw the angel in the marble and carved until I set him free." When asked how he made his statue, Michelangelo is reported to have said, "It is easy. You just chip away the stone that doesn't look like David."

After a two-hour wait in a long line of tourists, I was about to see it for myself. I stopped just inside the narrow corridor, still thirty feet from the *David*. This was not where everyone else wanted to stop and so I caused a bit of a traffic jam.

I understood why everyone rushed past me. Why would anyone stop to stare at the unfinished sculptures lining the hallway? Why attend to blocks of stone with roughly hewn, half-completed figures when sculpted perfection stands just a short walk away? Who would stop?

Some prisons don't require bars to keep people locked inside. All it takes is their perception that they belong there.

A woman captivated by seeing her interior reality vividly depicted in stone, that's who. I stood in the shadow of one of the unfinished sculptures that's part of this collection aptly titled, *Prisoners*. And I stared.

I tilted my head and let it soak in. This less-noticed sculpture was me—an unfinished prisoner locked away in a hard place.

Then I turned and looked down the corridor at the *David*, the statue fully chiseled by a master artist. As I walked toward it, I whispered, "O God, chisel me. I don't want to be locked in my hard places forever. I want to be free. I want to be all that You have in mind for me to be."

It is beautiful when the Master chisels. God doesn't want us to label ourselves and stay stuck. But He does want to make us aware of the chiseling that needs to be done. So instead of condemning myself with statements like, *I'm such a mess*, I could say, *Let God chisel. Let Him work on my hard places so I can leave the dark places of being stuck and come into the light of who He designed me to be.*

God is calling us out—out of darkness, out from those places we thought would never get better, out of being stuck. And with His call comes His promise that He will complete the good work He began in us (Philippians 1:6).

Lord, You are the Divine Artist. Thank You for applying Your creativity to me—first in creating me, and now in continuing to shape me into who You designed me to be. I surrender to Your work. In Jesus' Name, Amen.

A Prayer from Lysa

*If you declare with your mouth, "Jesus is Lord," and believe in
your heart that God raised him from the dead, you will be saved.*
—Romans 10:9

When I was in my early twenties, I felt very distant from God. A
series of heartbreaking situations in my life made me question
His goodness and whether or not He really loved me. But through
His divine grace, eventually truth broke through my cold resistance
and brought me to the place where I wanted to accept His love and
dedicate my life to Him.

The challenge was that I didn't know how to do this and I was too
afraid to ask my friends. As I remembered struggling through this
years ago, I wondered if you might be facing this same struggle too.
Maybe you've had some ups and downs with this whole God thing but
finally you're in a place where you want to give your heart to Him,
accept His grace, and receive salvation.

If that's you, I'd like to invite you to pray this salvation prayer with
me today:

> *Dear God,*
>
> *Thank You for the gift of grace and forgiveness. Thank You that
> in the midst of my sin, You have made a way, through Jesus, to forgive
> my sin and make me right with You.*
>
> *So today I confess my sinfulness . . . my hard heart . . . my mean*

thoughts . . . my harsh words . . . my doubt. I believe with all my heart that it was for me—and because of me—that Jesus died.

Please forgive me of all my sin. Big sins. Small sins. Past sins. Present sins. And all sins to come. I exchange my sin for Jesus' goodness and holiness. By the shed blood of Jesus, I am now forgiven and free! Thank You that in this moment, You have sealed me with Your Holy Spirit. I receive this precious gift and trust You will do as You promise and make me a new creation, molding and shaping me from the inside out to be more like You!

I celebrate that the old me is gone and the new me is here to stay! I love You and am forever grateful for Your forgiveness and my new life in You. I ask all this in Jesus' Name. Amen.

I love you, dear friend. And I'm rejoicing with all of heaven over every decision made to accept God's free gift of salvation. It truly is the sweetest gift we'll ever receive.

CONNECTING GOD'S HEART TO YOURS: 31 PERSONALIZED SCRIPTURES FOR EACH DAY

*W*hen God feels far away or seemingly silent, we must remember that His written Word is always available to us. In fact, Hebrews 4:12 tells us the Bible is "alive and active."

One of my favorite things to do with Scripture is place my name in a verse to make it feel more personalized. Like a love note sent from God's heart to mine. That's why I've put together a list of 31 scriptures, one for each day of the month, so you'll have this intimate connection with Him daily.

I anointed you, {insert name here}, set My seal of ownership on you, and put My Spirit in your heart as a deposit, guaranteeing what is to come. 2 CORINTHIANS 1:21–22

Since you are in Christ, {insert name here}, I have made you an heir of all My promises. GALATIANS 3:29

Neither height nor depth, nor anything else in all creation, will be able to separate you, {insert name here}, from My love that is in Christ Jesus. ROMANS 8:39

Because of Jesus, you, {insert name here}, are free from all condemnation. ROMANS 8:1

My plan for your future, {insert name here}, is filled with hope. JEREMIAH 29:11

I will take hold of your hand, {insert name here}, to keep you from falling. PSALM 37:24

My power will rest on you, {insert name here}, when you are weak. 2 CORINTHIANS 12:9

In Christ, you, are a new creation, {insert name here}. The old has gone, the new is here! 2 CORINTHIANS 5:17

Cast all your worries on Me, {insert name here}, for I really care about you. 1 PETER 5:7

It is for freedom that Christ has set you free, {insert name here}. Do not let yourself be burdened again by a yoke of slavery. GALATIANS 5:1

My love for you,
{insert name here},
will persevere through
every situation.
1 CORINTHIANS 13:4–7

Not one of My promises
will ever fail you,
{insert name here}.
JOSHUA 23:14

For as high as the heavens are above the earth,
so great is My steadfast love toward you, {insert
name here}. As far as the east is from the west,
I remove your transgressions. PSALM 103:11–12

For you are My handiwork, {insert name here},
created in Christ Jesus to do good works, which I
prepared in advance for you to do. EPHESIANS 2:10

Trust in Me with all your
heart, {insert name here},
and I will guide you.
PROVERBS 3:5–6

I will give you peace,
{insert name here},
at all times and in
every situation.
2 THESSALONIANS 3:16

Now in Christ Jesus you, {insert name here}, who once was far away has been brought near by the blood of Christ. EPHESIANS 2:13

Call on Me, {insert name here}, when you are in trouble and I will rescue you. PSALM 91:15

My peace, which transcends all understanding, will guard your heart and your mind in Christ Jesus, {insert name here}. PHILIPPIANS 4:7

I will keep you safe, {insert name here}, because no one can snatch you out of My hand. JOHN 10:29

I will meet all your needs, {insert name here}, according to the riches of My glory in Christ Jesus. PHILIPPIANS 4:19

In Christ you have been brought to fullness, {insert name here}. He is the head over every power and authority. COLOSSIANS 2:10

You can know and depend on the love that I have for you, {insert name here}.

1 JOHN 4:16

You can trust in Me, {insert name here}, for I will never forsake you.

PSALM 9:10

I will rejoice over you with gladness, {insert name here}. I will quiet you with My love. ZEPHANIAH 3:17

Since you have been raised with Christ, {insert name here}, set your heart on things above, where Christ is, seated at My right hand. COLOSSIANS 3:1

Though the mountains vanish, My unending love will never leave you, {insert name here}.

ISAIAH 54:10

My grace was poured out on you abundantly, {insert name here}, along with the faith and love that are in Christ Jesus.

1 TIMOTHY 1:14

I see all your hardships, {insert name here},

and I care about your suffering. Psalm 31:7

I will protect and carry

you, {insert name here},

all the days of your life.

Isaiah 46:4

I made you alive in Jesus

simply because I love

you, {insert name here}.

Ephesians 2:4–5

(For a printable version of these verses and
instructions for how to make a scripture box, visit
http://www.proverbs31.org/personal-scriptures.)

Notes

Chapter: Is God Good to Me?

1. "C. S. Lewis Quotes, Quotable Quotes," Good Reads, accessed February 22, 2016, http://www.goodreads.com/quotes/615-we-are-not-necessarily -doubting-that-god-will-do-the.

Chapter: The Scribbled Truth That Changed My Life

1. Lysa TerKeurst, *Finding I AM: How Jesus Fully Satisfies the Cry of Your Heart* (Nashville, TN: LifeWay Press, 2017), 92–93.

Index

Topics

DEVOTIONS

ABOUT THE AUTHOR

*L*ysa is a wife to Art and mom to five priority blessings named Jackson, Mark, Hope, Ashley, and Brooke. She is the president of Proverbs 31 Ministries and author of twenty-one books, including the *New York Times* bestsellers *Uninvited, The Best Yes, Unglued,* and *Made to Crave.* Additionally, Lysa has been featured on *Focus on the Family, The Today Show, Good Morning America,* and more. Lysa speaks nationwide at Catalyst, Lifeway Abundance Conference, Women of Joy, and various church events.

To those who know her best, Lysa is simply a woman who loves Jesus passionately, is dedicated to her family, and struggles like the rest of us with laundry, junk drawers, and cellulite.

Connect with Lysa on a daily basis, follow her speaking schedule, and receive biblical encouragement:

Blog: www.LysaTerKeurst.com
Facebook: www.Facebook.com/OfficialLysa
Instagram: @LysaTerKeurst
Twitter: @LysaTerKeurst

About Proverbs 31 Ministries

*L*ysa TerKeurst is the president of Proverbs 31 Ministries, located in Charlotte, North Carolina.

If you were inspired by *Embraced* and desire to deepen your own personal relationship with Jesus Christ, we have just what you're looking for.

Proverbs 31 Ministries exists to be a trusted friend who will take you by the hand and walk by your side, leading you one step closer to the heart of God through:

Free First 5 app
Free online daily devotions
Online Bible studies
Writer and speaker training
Daily radio programs
Books and resources

For more information about Proverbs 31 Ministries, visit www.Proverbs31.org.

To inquire about having Lysa speak at your event, visit www.LysaTerKeurst.com and click on "speaking."

ALSO AVAILABLE FROM LYSA TERKEURST

Am I Messing Up My Kids? . . . and Other Questions Every Mom Asks

Becoming More Than a Good Bible Study Girl

The Best Yes: Making Wise Decisions in the Midst of Endless Demands

Finding I AM: How Jesus Fully Satisfies the Cry of Your Heart

*It Will Be Okay: Trusting God Through Fear
and Change (Little Seed & Little Fox)*

Made to Crave: Satisfying Your Deepest Desire with God, Not Food

Unglued: Making Wise Choices in the Midst of Raw Emotions

Uninvited: Living Loved When You Feel Less Than, Left Out, and Lonely

*What Happens When Women Say Yes to God:
Experiencing Life in Extraordinary Ways*

*What Happens When Women Walk in Faith:
Trusting God Takes You to Amazing Places*

Win or Lose, I Love You! (Lulu and Her Tutu)

*The Enemy wants us to feel rejected . . .
left out, lonely, and less than.*

In *Uninvited*, Lysa shares her own deeply personal experiences and leans in to honestly examine the roots of rejection, as well as rejection's ability to poison relationships from the inside out, including our relationship with God.

With biblical depth, gut-honest vulnerability, and refreshing wit, Lysa will help you:

- Stop feeling left out by believing that even when you are overlooked by others you are handpicked by God.
- Change your tendency to either fall apart or control the actions of others by embracing God-honoring ways to process your hurt.
- Know exactly what to pray for the next ten days to steady your soul and restore your confidence in the midst of rejection.
- Overcome the two core fears that feed your insecurities by understanding the secret of belonging.

Get a copy of the book, study guide, and DVD wherever books are sold or by visiting www.uninvitedbook.com.

Are you living with the stress of an overwhelmed schedule and aching with the sadness of an underwhelmed soul?

Lysa TerKeurst is learning that there is a big difference between saying yes to everyone and saying yes to God. In *The Best Yes* she will help you:

- Cure the disease to please with a biblical understanding of the command to love.
- Escape the guilt of disappointing others by learning the secret of the small no.
- Overcome the agony of hard choices by embracing a wisdom based decision-making process.
- Rise above the rush of endless demands and discover your Best Yes today.

Get a copy of the book, study guide, and DVD wherever books are sold or by visiting www.thebestyes.com.

The free app you've been looking for!
Give God your first thoughts every day.

We say we put God first... so wouldn't it make sense that we give Him the first 5 minutes of each day? That's why Proverbs 31 Ministries created the First 5 app. With First 5, you will:

• Honor God by letting His truth direct your first thoughts of the day and discover how much healthier your perspective of life becomes.

• Discover unique parts of the Bible you may have missed by studying one verse in one chapter, one day at a time.

• Replace feelings of comparison and rejection that social media often brings by starting your day with the truth of God's Word.

• Gain confidence in your ability to navigate Scripture by learning to identify the major moments in each chapter.

Download the app for FREE!

FIRST5.ORG